Advance Praise for
101+ Ways to Help Israel

"Over the years, I have been asked again and again, 'How can I help Israel.' This book is an indispensable guide that answers that question with good humor and great passion, with subtlety and soul. Thanks to Haskell Nussbaum for helping us all stand up for – and celebrate – the miracle of Israel."

GIL TROY, Professor of History, McGill University and author of *Why I Am a Zionist: Israel, Jewish Identity and the Challenges of Today*.

"Haskell Nussbaum's 101+ Ways to Help Israel is a timely and vital resource for supporters of Israel who want to get involved with celebrating its 60th anniversary and beyond."

DAVID BRINN, Founding Editorial Director, ISRAEL21c.

"A journey of a thousand miles begins with the first step; and as all Jews are responsible for each other, every contribution – however small – to Israel's security and survival is a '*mitzva*'. In the 37 years I have lived in Jerusalem, I have seen wars, terrorist attacks, the agony of families who lost their loved ones, the injustice of a biased foreign media.

"Haskell Nussbaum is doing a great '*mitzva*' in showing our brethren, wherever they may live, how to help in Israel's ongoing battle against the forces trying to destroy her. It is a book to read, to share with friends, to use to motivate yourself into action. I wish the author every success, because his message needs to be heard."

DVORA WAYSMAN, author of 10 books including *The Pomegranate Pendant, Seeds of the Pomegranate, Esther*, and *Woman of Jerusalem*. Waysman is syndicated world-wide and has won several literary prizes.

"For the average person who has occasionally wondered what he/she can do to help Israel to the hard-core Israel activist, Haskell Nussbaum's book is a treasure trove of creative suggestions and meaningful outlets to aid the Jewish State. A short read that can have a long term impact."

DAVID BOROWICH, Founder and Honorary Chairman, Dor Chadash and Co-Chairman, Israel and International Affairs Commission of the Jewish Community Relations Council of NY.

Praise for
Beat That Parking Ticket

"I never thought I'd enjoy a book about parking tickets so much!"
SUSAN JUHN, NY1

A comprehensive guide [and] a very funny book.
ROB MORRISON, Today in New York

Beat That Parking Ticket is [Nussbaum's] gift to New Yorkers.
BROOKLYN EAGLE

101+ Ways to Help Israel

HASKELL NUSSBAUM

101+ WAYS TO HELP ISRAEL

A Guide to Doing Small Things That Can Make Big Differences

Gavel Press
New York

Published by Gavel Press, P.O. Box 20432, New York, NY, 10001-0008, U.S.A.

www.gavelpress.com

This book is available at quantity discounts for bulk purchases. For orders or further information contact info@gavelpress.com.

Graphic Design: Eva Katz

ISBN 10: 0-9786825-4-8
ISBN 13: 978-0-9786825-4-5

Publisher's CIP Data
Nussbaum, Haskell.
101+ ways to help israel: a guide to doing small things that can make big differences / by Haskell Nussbaum.
    p   cm.
ISBN 10: 0-9786825-4-8
ISBN 13: 978-0-9786825-4-5
1. Israel –History.   2. Arab-Israeli conflict.   3. Zionism   I. Title

DS125 2008   Library of Congress Control Number: 2008901483
956.94 dc22

Printed in the United States of America.

10 9 8 7 6 5 4 3 2 1

Visit this book's website at: **WaysToHelpIsrael.com**

To my wife, for her unflagging support.

Table of Contents

PART 1

THE BASICS

1. Introduction – Why This Book

This is a guide book for those of us who don't (presently) live in Israel but who nevertheless care about Israel's long-term survival and want to contribute.

Contributing to Israel can be a hard or an easy mission. It can be as difficult as picking up your entire life and moving there or as easy as dropping a few coins into a charity box. This book is primarily for people who are not going to turn their entire lives upside down for the Jewish State, but who are willing to spend at least a few minutes each day – or each week, or even month – to help Israel not only survive, but thrive, for centuries to come.

Yes, I said centuries. For unlike books about Israeli politics, this book is not about borders, military options, or all the government policies that people agree with or disagree with. On the contrary. Every suggestion in this book is meant to help Israel carry on for generations to come – no matter who your great-grandchildren ultimately vote for.

I believe in the power of individuals. And I believe in the power of small contributions to ripple into large differences. Although some of the suggestions in this book are difficult or time consuming, most are not. The goal was to produce a book full of suggestions that can be easily incorporated into our lives, while still providing a comprehensive guide for those people and activists who have more time to invest. To that end, I tried to make this book as complete a reference book as possible, while still keeping it a light read, easy to digest in small pieces.

Whether you're Jewish, Christian, Moslem or Hindi, an ardent activist, an aspiring (or inspiring) philanthropist or an armchair General, I hope that this book helps you find new activities, discover new friendships, expand your experiences and generally find a few more pebbles to throw to create those ripples that will support Israel's very existence.

A SHORT GUIDE TO USING THIS BOOK

The key to using this book is to search for ideas by subject and activity. Thus, if you're looking, for example, for ways to help Israel while you're at work, you can turn to the **At Work and As Communities** section and there you will find suggestions geared for ordinary workers, business owners and anyone who works with or for a non profit organization. If you're a parent looking for activities to do with your children, you can find most of those in the section labeled **The Next Generation**.

Although I tried to keep the ideas for activities distinct, there will often be times where it pays to look at more than one section. A student, for example, might want to look at both the **Campus Activism** section and the more general **Social and Leisure Activities** section to find suitable ideas.

In addition, each chapter generally begins with the easier suggestions, followed by ideas that require more time or effort. Thus, someone looking for a quick idea can stop earlier in the chapter, while someone looking to, say, organize an ongoing project for themselves or their community, might start by flipping to the middle or end of any given chapter.

Finally, each chapter ends with a **Things You Can Do Today** section, meant to be a quick at-a-glance recap of the ideas suggested in that chapter.

2. Being a Spokesperson for Israel's Right to Exist

We were sitting around the dining room table in my apartment in Jerusalem and the arguments were getting heated. I tended to like debating so I would deliberately invite people who were so far left that they wouldn't even drink water that came from the Golan Heights and sit them next to people who lived in tiny settlements in the West Bank, the kind where there were more guns in the town than people. Politics in Israel was, for all of us, intensely important and relevant, potentially life-changing and (for me, at least) a great dinner-table sport.

It was a good time for a fight. The Oslo Agreement had not yet been ratified by the Knesset, there were demonstrations and counter-demonstrations galore, and everyone was certain that they knew best what the country should do. Even as I went to the kitchen to bring out the chicken and salads I could see faces around the table turning shades of red as they strained to convince equally stubborn opponents of their arguments. When I saw that one of my friends was turning more purple than the red cabbage, I decided to intervene and cool tempers down.

Easier said than done. My purple-faced friend was frothing, the woman he was arguing with was a breath away from leaving the table in disgust and everyone had stopped eating completely. I could tell that only a genuine diversion would do, so I did something "drastic" and let my elbow knock the bottle of red wine right over onto the table. As everyone abruptly had to scramble to save their outfits, the tension broke. With a rueful laugh, the cabbage-hued man backed down and cracked a joke, the woman was happy to avoid any staining splashes and we avoided politics for the rest of the night.

Avoiding politics is part of my goal in this book, too, and especially in this chapter. When it comes to being a spokesperson for Israel the only presumption that I'm working on is that you support the very basic right that Israel deserves to exist at all. Regardless of what you think about its government's policies.

It is a sad truth that Israel has enemies that wish it would disappear completely. And it is a blunt reality that one of the sharpest arrows in their quill is the spreading popularity of the idea that Israel lacks the very legitimacy to exist. This is an idea which exists outside of any Israeli policy.

We are creatures who strive for consistency and when an idea enters our heads and takes root, it branches out to control our actions. If the notion that Israel was founded illegitimately and its continued existence is wrongful to the Arab nation takes hold over a majority of the West's population then Israel will be in serious trouble. Quite simply, Israel will lack allies willing to take any action on its behalf (especially potentially risky action) in any time of need.

Israel is a tiny country and it needs its allies behind her, both for military purposes and for continued access to trade and energy sources. The country is just too small to go it alone. And, absent a future discovery of major oil fields, this need for the outside world is, shall we say, less than equally reciprocated.

So, regardless of where our politics lie in terms of solving the Arab-Israeli conflict, we should all agree that there is a real need to bolster support for Israel's very right to exist – even in countries such as the U.S., where the level of support for Israel is generally high.

Fortunately, this is an area where all of us can shine. Each one of us, irrespective of our oratorical skills or erudition, can become an effective spokesperson for Israel's right to exist – and we can do it without breaking the bank or spewing propaganda.

Let's start with one simple idea:

Israelis Are Not Marketing Geniuses

Israelis are known for many commendable traits including creativity, innovation, bravery and a willingness to speak their minds (sometimes some of us would rather they stop speaking their minds...). But they can't be everywhere, they generally speak Hebrew, a language spoken nowhere else, and their idea of spreading a message often seems to be that if they think they're right they assume everyone else will think so too.

As people living outside of Israel, we know our surroundings and our cultures better and more intimately than most Israelis ever could. It is, therefore, an utter waste of time to complain about Israel's less-than-stellar job at PR and start taking on the work ourselves.

And now that that's out of the way, let's get started.

First: Learn the Issues

It's not always a picnic to bone up on history and geo-politics (though if you're like me, you may enjoy it). But if you aren't already familiar with the Balfour Declaration, the British Mandatory period, the 1922 League of Nations decision regarding Palestine, the creation of TransJordan, the 1947 UN Partition Plan, the Ottoman Empire, the various waves of Aliyah, Mark Twain's description of Palestine in the 19th century, the Bible, the migratory patterns of Jews and Arabs after World War I and

II, the Six Day War, the founding of the PLO and its Charter, and the basic politics and geography of the modern State of Israel – well, what can I say: there's always more to learn, isn't there? And, luckily, there are plenty of resources available (see the resources list at the back of the book) to help you delve as deeply as you are interested.

Is it really necessary, you may ask, to become an expert just to defend Israel's basic right to exist?

Well, no. But here's a thought: If you undertake to learn even just one new fact about Israel every week, the impact over time could be life-changing. And your words will carry more authority You will, in fact, *become* an expert.

On the assumption, though, that most people like immediate and short answers to even the toughest of questions, here's what I think is the very least that can be said about Israel's basic right to exist: the Jews started immigrating to the land, in numbers, during the Ottoman Empire, built up the land under the auspices of the League of Nations, fought for it after the Arabs rejected the UN Partition Plan and have developed it into a modern state, with one vote per citizen regardless of race. Settling the land, developing it with sweat and blood and allowing everyone to vote – why, it sounds downright American, doesn't it?

And that's not even mentioning all the historical or religious arguments.

But on the subject of Israel's beginnings, let's move on to another facet of defending Israel.

Did You Know?

Israel, at approximately 8,000 square miles
(not including the West Bank) is 1/640th the size
of the lands of the 22 Arab States, 1/19th the size
of California, and around the same size as New Jersey
or Vancouver Island (in Canada). To see this visually,
check out www.iris.org.il/sizemaps.htm.

Respond to Propaganda

There are plenty of actions by Israelis and loads of policies of
the Israeli government (both present and past) that reasonable
people can disagree with. Similarly, there are many sides to the
question of where to draw borders, what parts of the West Bank
(if any) Israel should hold on to, and all the questions surrounding the Israeli-Palestinian conflict that swirl about in a moral
miasma.

When it comes to politics, even reasonable people have been
known to get, er, feisty.

Most of that isn't propaganda. Respond only if you like debates.
But certain phrases are really disguised fighting words. When
someone says that Zionism is racism, when solutions to the
Israeli-Palestinian conflict supposedly must include a Palestinian
right of return to all of Israel and when Arabs claim that
Jerusalem never really had a Jewish Temple – these are all
codes for saying that Israel has no right to exist.

For these arguments, you must arm yourself with knowledge
(check out the resources list in the back of this book) and
respond accordingly. It's perfectly normal, for instance, to
empathize with the pain of a Palestinian refugee – who can deny
that wars result in terrible unfairness perpetrated on innocents?
But there were many wars in the 20th century and millions upon
millions of refugees as a result. Whatever your thoughts about a

Palestinian state in the West Bank and Gaza Strip, one doesn't have to *destroy* Israel to solve this issue.

And now that the heavy stuff is out of the way, let's move on to something lighter.

There is, however, one source you can rely on when it comes to keeping track of news stories on the Middle East – CAMERA – Committee for Accuracy in Middle East Reporting in America.
Ed Koch, former mayor of New York

Shining a Positive Light on Israel in Any Capacity Helps

Any time someone sees something about Israel, or about Israelis, that makes them smile, the country benefits. Telling a friend about an Israeli medical breakthrough that you read about online, watching an Israeli movie, or even hanging up a poster or calendar of lovely Israeli male or female eye-candy – all of these simple things can help re-enforce a positive image of Israel. Believe it or not, these things help with the argument over Israel's right to exist.

Which brings us to:

Start With Your Circle of Influence

The best place to be a spokesperson for Israel is on and around the trails that we walk every day anyway. In school, at work, during conferences that we attend, at union meetings, visiting online groups, or even on the bus or subway.

There are a myriad of ways of supporting Israel's right to exist without being preachy; below are a few ideas to help get you started.

Put a Pro-Israel Bumper Sticker on Your Car

Bumper stickers, mugs that sit on your desk, t-shirts, hats and buttons on your knapsack – all are great ways of passively showing support for Israel or displaying an upbeat statement or image of Israel, while broadcasting that you're available to answer questions for those who are interested.

Pass Along E-mails

Less passively, consider sending or forwarding an apolitical e-mail about Israel to a co-worker or friend, once every few months. E-mails that link to articles that highlight Israel as a leading-edge technology power or as a democracy are clearly good candidates (for some ideas, read Israeli websites such as **www.israel21c.org**). Online petitions that inherently have as a premise that Israel has the right to exist might be worthwhile, too, depending on how active or political you want to get.

Recommend Books

People are often looking for new books to read. Recommend some pro-Israel ones or a novel set in or about Israel (see the resources list at the back of the book or start with **Exodus** by Leon Uris). Additionally, you can donate or recommend these books to your local schools or libraries (talk to the acquisitions librarian next time you're there, if you want to do this).

Fly an Israeli Flag

Everyone ought to display an Israeli flag on **Israel's Independence Day**. Whether you fly it from your porch or car, mount it on a small paperweight planted on your desk at work, or pin it on your lapel, a flag is a quick and easy way of supporting Israel. If you want to be more proactive, give out small flags to friends and co-workers on **Israel's Independence Day** and ask them to fly it for a day.

Expand Your Circle of Influence

Now would also be a good time to expand your circle of influence. Make friends with the journalist covering the local beat, the publicists at your company, the professors at your college (regardless of the subjects they are teaching). These are people who routinely come into contact with influential people in our world. Passing along a good book or having a brief conversation about Israel can have a great ripple effect down the road.

Top Ten Ways to Help Israel that Take 5 Minutes or Less:

1. Put a pro-Israel bumper sticker on your car.
2. Hang up an Israeli poster or painting on a wall.
3. Put a charity box for an Israeli charity in your place of business.
4. Add a website link to an Israeli site on your own website. Or send a link to your friends.
5. Read the headlines of an Israeli newspaper.
6. Decide to spend $10 a month on Israeli products. Then buy an Israeli product online.
7. Ask your local video store to stock Israeli titles.
8. Listen to an Israeli song in your car.
9. Order Israeli take-out food.
10. Put a tiny amount of money aside for a trip to Israel next year.

Bonus #11: Buy a copy of this book for a friend!

In short, decide to be an advocate for Israel's right to exist. Whether you follow politics or not, there are many small ways that you can make big differences in this oh-so-important area.

THINGS YOU CAN DO TODAY:

1. Decide to become a spokesperson for Israel's right to exist within your circle of influence.
2. Learn one new fact every week. Read a page of a book, find an article online, go to a lecture, join an online group, read an Israeli paper, like the **Jerusalem Post** or **Haaretz** (both of which are available in English), subscribe to or read online **dailyalert.org**. Check the resources in this book for more ideas.
3. Respond to anti-Israel propaganda when you hear it. If you're feeling proactive, look for it in the media or online or sign up for email reports from groups like **CAMERA** or **honestreporting.org**, or the **Anti-Defamation League**.
4. Hang up an Israeli calendar. It can be flowers, landscapes, historical photos with links to the Bible, or, yes, even something racy.
5. Go online and search for positive items about Israeli innovations (use a search engine) and then tell people around you about them.
6. Rent an Israeli video (it doesn't have to be political). Try **Ushpizin** or **Salah Shabati**. Invite some friends or your neighbors or co-workers over and make a night of it.
7. Put a pro-Israel bumper sticker on your car.
8. Donate or recommend pro-Israel books to your local schools or libraries.
9. Check for anti-Israel resolutions on your campus or by your union.
10. Find and distribute articles (start by searching online sites such as **www.israel21c.org**) that highlight Israel's achievements. These can be indirect, too. Hanging them up at work or at school can be a great conversation starter.
11. Talk to people at school or work about Israel, in a non-threatening way. Remember to listen at least as much as you talk.

12. Recommend books (nonfiction, or novels such as **Exodus** by Leon Uris) that show Israelis as normal non-demonic people to your friends and co-workers. You might want to try some Israeli writers who have been translated into English, too.
13. Sign online petitions that you agree with, that have as a premise that Israel has the right to exist.
14. Fly an Israeli flag on Israel's Independence Day.
15. Brainstorm with your friends and family about ways to make your local community more aware of Israel as a democracy.
16. Talk to journalists, PR people, lawyers, accountants, professors and others who routinely interact with many people – and expand your circle of influence. Don't start with Israel-related subjects – build a relationship first.

PART 2

SOCIAL AND LEISURE ACTIVITIES

3. Bringing in Israeli Arts and Culture

Politics, shmolitics – if you want to imbue a warm feeling towards Israel in someone who's never been there, what quicker way than to bring them a taste of Israeli art, culture – or even food?

This is surely one of the least controversial ways of reaching people who may otherwise not care less about Israel – and turning them into advocates for Israel's existence by the simple act of having them identify with and appreciate Israelis.

Take 'em Out to the Movies

Hands down the quickest and easiest way to bring the sounds and sights of living in Israel into your local neighborhood is by screening an Israeli movie. Whether you rent a DVD, go to a local event at an organization supporting Israel or wait for the annual Israeli Film Festival – make it your business to see at least one movie a year with someone who has never been to Israel. Even if you don't follow it up with an Israel-related discussion over a cup of coffee, you'll have helped the country.

> *I want to continue the growth of the festival and continue bringing exposure to all of the talented hard-working Israeli filmmakers.*
> **Meir Fenigstein,**
> **director of the Israel Film Festival**

This may also be an opportunity, by the way, to lobby your nearest video store to stock (more) Israeli titles. Do an online search for Israeli comedies, for instance, and suggest at least two or three possibilities to the local manager. (The movie **Ushpizin** is a good example, and the Israeli classic **Salah Shabati** stars Topol – the actor who starred in Fiddler on the Roof).

The Sound of (Israeli) Music

Whether you buy a CD, download music from the internet or hum it yourself, exposing someone to Israeli music is a great way to get them to like something about the country.

Fortunately, there's something for everyone when it comes to Israeli music – there are bands and singers that sound like American rock stars, others who are indistinguishable from the best Arabic crooners and still others who would appeal to a Latin audience. And for the upscale audience there are classics performed by the Israeli Philharmonic, including symphonies conducted by the famous Zubin Mehta.

Get a hold of some tunes you like and send them to coworkers and friends. Or keep a CD in your car and play it when you offer someone a ride home. What could be easier?

A Picture is Worth a Thousand...

Paintings, sketch drawings, photographs – show an appreciative person the right visual image and that person might just remember it for the rest of his or her life. Make it the right image of Israel or by an Israeli and you've done the country a real favor.

Luckily, there are plenty of pictures that are worth a look if you're interested in Israel. Whether you go to a museum, art gallery, photography exhibition or just e-mail someone a slide show, there are options for almost anyone's taste. Check out local shows and the internet for visiting exhibitions – and if there aren't any coming up, well isn't that just a cry for help? Call the museum or art gallery yourself and start pestering them about when they will have an Israeli section added. Or at least one or two samples, in a temporary exhibit.

Top Ten Ways to Help Israel from Your Living Room:

1. Invite an Israeli to dinner.
2. Rent an Israeli video and invite your friends and neighbors. Serve Israeli snacks.
3. Start a book club for books about Israel or by Israeli writers.
4. Throw a fundraising party. The key is to make them fun, so that people won't mind paying the admission charge. Maybe combine it with a contest for the best cake or pie.
5. Subscribe to an Israeli magazine or newspaper. Or read one online.
6. Talk to your family about one Israel-related topic at dinner each night. Research the subject ahead of time.
7. Listen to Israeli music, taped or via the internet. Or watch an Israeli channel, if one is offered.
8. Take a virtual tour of Israel, online.
9. Organize informal seminars, where you invite your friends and family to hear a speaker talk about current events in Israel, over dinner or coffee.
10. Hang up Israeli art.

Curl Up with an Israeli Book

If you want to immerse yourself in Israeli ideas and thoughts, or if you want to introduce a friend to the mindset of ordinary (and extraordinary) Israelis, the simplest thing to do is to pick up a book. Whether it's a book *about* Israel or, better yet, *by* an Israeli writer, reading is the fast-track to becoming a true connoisseur of Israeli culture (see the resources list at the back of the book if you'd like a few suggestions).

Once you've chosen a book (or two, or three), don't just read it when you're huddled, alone, in the corner of your fenced-in backyard. Take it with you to work, read it on the bus and subway, recommend it to strangers, start a book-club and discuss it with a group, suggest it when you go on dates – make your voice heard. You might also want to recommend it to your local library as a suggestion to put on their "recommended" shelves.

The Power of Online Culture

Whether it's listening to Israeli radio stations or TV programs online, visiting online Israeli galleries, finding cool Israeli websites, learning Hebrew online, or just surfing through Israeli news – it's never been easier to bring a taste of Israeli culture right to your desktop at home or at work (and see the resources list at the back of the book for a few quick suggested sites).

Throw a Party

Speaking of tastes of Israel – why not throw a party with an Israeli theme? Order (or make) Israeli food, put on Israeli music (or hire a band), and serve Israeli wine. If you're going for an upscale feel – why, make it an Israeli wine and cheese party! Unlike yesteryear, today Israel boasts many award-winning wines and a huge variety of cheese delicacies.

Alternatively, if an all-out Israeli party seems over the top, then perhaps just bringing a bottle of Israeli wine to your boss or to a dinner party could be a great conversation starter too.

Jangle Some Jewelry and Other Visual Stimulants

Bracelets, necklaces and rings from Israel can be great conversation pieces (and can be bought online or in Judaica stores, if you don't happen to have a trip to Israel planned for the near future) and the same goes for putting up an Israeli poster on your wall, framing an Israeli painting, using some Israeli ceramics (for decoration or as utensils) or even displaying pricey Israeli artifacts (such as ancient coins or oil lamps). Even a small picture on your desk with Jerusalem in the background is sure to gather attention.

Order an Israeli Channel

If it's available in your area, through satellite or cable, consider ordering any Israeli channel being offered. News, movies, TV programming – it's all there at the click of a remote. Besides entertainment, it might also be a good way of learning Hebrew.

Take a Dance Class

Whether you do it alone or (better) with a friend, consider taking a class in Israeli dance. It's fun, you'll get a workout and you'll identify with Israelis – all at once.

Did You Know?

Operas are sometimes held in the amphitheater in Caesaria, the same theater used by the Romans nearly 2000 years ago.

Teach Kids

Speaking of classes, teaching kids to appreciate Israeli culture is a great way to get the next generation to connect. Introducing an Israeli novelist to a literature class, paintings to an art class, or even poetry to aspiring poets (think **Haim Bialik**) ought to be relatively easy to implement. If not in school, then in after-school classes and workshops. Or even to the kid next door, completely informally.

Similarly, if your kids are already involved in an activity (such as summer camp or after-school workshops), suggest to the administrators and teachers that adding an Israeli component would be both fun and educational. The more concrete your suggestion (a specific book, play, painting to copy) the more likely they are to include it.

Hire a Band

Here's a great proactive idea: Find a band and have a live performance of Israeli music. Whether you go all out and fly in an Israeli singer or whether you find someone local to play some tunes, a live event gives you the chance to invite multiple friends and coworkers and enjoy the sounds of Israel at a local club or café.

Publicize Israeli Artists

When Israeli artists are in town, send out e-mails to everyone and include local papers. In fact, a good idea is to recommend Israeli artists to local journalists, whether to be reviewed or to be used for profiles and other features.

Invite an Israeli Author

If you're serious about Israeli books, it's a good idea to try to get in touch with Israeli writers and journalists and invite them to speak at local events, or to local organizations. Chances are they'll jump at the opportunity and you can then bring a date or a colleague to hear them – fusing a chance to connect to Israeli culture with a chance to make yourself look like a mover and shaker to your friends.

Translate Hebrew Articles and Books

If you really want to be impressive in the literary arena, you can even find Israeli articles and books in Hebrew and have them translated and distributed locally – legally, of course. Just call the magazine or publisher and talk to the rights department. (Business idea, anyone?)

Hold a Contest

One way of exposing children to culture, while making it fun, is by holding a contest, giving prizes for the best drawings, essays, photos or websites dealing with Israel. Kids are so creative, it'll be a sheer joy to judge the entries.

If you're feeling particularly energetic, try to get a local business to sponsor the contest (make it a wider one than just your own children and your friends') and then call the local paper to try to garner some publicity.

Put on a Play

If you have a group of kids (or even adults) and some time on your hands, you might want to think about putting on a play. This can be as elaborate or as simple as you like. There are several Israeli plays that can be used (see the resources list at the back of the book) or you can challenge people to write their own. One piece of advice, if you go this route: keep the play(s) relatively short, to make life easier.

A Few Resources for Israeli Culture:

- http://ilmuseums.com
- www.israelfilmfestival.com
- www.israelartguide.co.il
- www.israel-music.com

For more resources check the resources list in the back of the book.

THINGS YOU CAN DO TODAY:

1. Rent or buy an Israeli movie and show it to your friends, family, colleagues etc.
2. Ask your local video store to stock Israeli titles.
3. Buy or burn a CD with Israeli music. Keep a copy in your car.
4. Go to a museum, art gallery or photo show featuring Israeli art. If you can't find one – suggest one to your local galleries or even businesses.
5. Contact Israeli museums and find out if they're doing local exhibitions in your area.
6. Read a book about Israel or by an Israeli author.
7. Send a slide-show of Israeli art to your friends who appreciate art; send video clips of Israeli music to those people who you think would like to hear them.
8. Tune in to an Israeli radio or TV station online.
9. Throw a party with an Israeli theme – straight food, or wine and cheese. Don't forget the Israeli music!
10. Wear Israeli jewelry.
11. Display Israeli artifacts, photos, and/or art on your desk at work.
12. Take a class in Israeli dance. Bring along a friend. Or a date.
13. Tell a child about Israel – by giving him or her a book, movie, music or suggesting a website.
14. Suggest Israeli components (books, artists, et al) to your kids' after-school classes and summer camps.
15. Buy some Israeli art online. Give Israeli jewelry as a gift.
16. Order an Israeli TV channel via your local Cable or Satellite provider.
17. Look for live bands playing music from Israel – or consider hiring one yourself. Perhaps the local café would be interested in co-sponsoring an event.
18. Find interesting articles about Israeli arts or oddities and distribute them to your friends. If you read Hebrew, peruse the Israeli press and translate the stories you think are interesting.
19. Book an Israeli band for your local university campus haunts.
20. Invite an Israeli writer or journalist to speak at a local event or organization or business meeting.

21. Hold a contest for the best essay, photo, website or painting relating to Israel. Try to get a local business to sponsor it and then call the local paper to give it some publicity.
22. Start a book club focusing on Israeli books.
23. Put on a play that has an Israeli character or that is set in Israel.
24. Suggest Israeli artists to local journalists – they can be used for profiles and other features, especially if they're visiting for a special reason.

4. Meeting Israelis Outside of Israel

When I touched down at Ben Gurion airport at the age of 16, I was a fiery idealistic Zionist who loved the country so much that the first thing I did was bend down and kiss the earth, right there, near a palm tree outside the arrivals gate. I didn't think it was corny (still don't); sometimes a land is so special it deserves a real expression of love.

Still, if you're anything like a normal person, you'd probably rather kiss your spouse or partner than a clump of dirt! No matter where that dirt lives (my luck, the patch I smooched was probably imported from overseas, along with the tree). Well, by the same token, it's far easier to relate to (and maybe even fall in love with) a real live Israeli than the land itself. Which is why I would posit that the easiest way to humanize Israel (and thus create support for its continued survival) is to arrange for people to interact with real, live Israelis.

And nowadays you don't have to go all the way to Israel to do that.

Find a Pen Pal

They're not as popular as they used to be, what with the internet taking over – but whether it's by snail mail or e-mail, if you hang out with Israelis and trade epistles, you can strike up some interesting friendships without ever leaving home. And the best

29

thing about this is that if you do ever visit Israel – maybe you'll have a free place to stay!

Make Israeli Friends

Wouldn't it be nice to hear the Israeli perspective on issues from actual three-dimensional Israelis? Of course, plenty of Israelis are rude, impatient, arrogant and ill-tempered (and those are the ones we like!) – but, seriously, speaking to Israelis for ten minutes will give you a better idea of how things work in the Middle East than 30 hours in a classroom. And most Israelis are happy to open up, even to strangers.

So how does one meet these Middle East mavens? Simple – you go looking for them. Israelis can be grouped into two categories for these purposes – those who are traveling and those who have decided to make homes outside of Israel.

Traveling Israelis include tourists, students and businesspeople – and besides trolling Madame Toussauds and other hot spots, you can try hopping over to the nearest Israeli consulate and keeping your eye out. Or, a better idea, approaching someone there about hiring an Israeli to speak at a private lunch, meeting or dinner.

But the easier way of making Israeli friends is to find some who are not living (at least right now) in Israel. And the best way to do that is to sign up for a Hebrew class. Even if you have little interest in actually studying the language, many of these classes are taught by Israelis and most Hebrew teachers know at least a few interesting characters.

Alternatively, one can hunt down these mythical creatures in Israeli restaurants, at synagogues (occasionally), and online (search for local organizations that cater to them, such as **www.dorchadashusa.org** in New York).

Did You Know?
The Bezalel school of art, in Jerusalem, is named after the Biblical Bezalel, who crafted the Menorah.

Find an Israeli Teacher

Whether it's to study Hebrew or a completely different topic, a good way to meet an Israeli and learn something at the same time is to take a class at a local college or institute where the professor is an Israeli. Or at least choose the Israeli teacher if you're weighing two courses, both of which interest you.

Talk in a Movie Theater

It's not usually polite to talk during a movie – but if it's an Israeli movie such as those in the Israeli film festivals, then it seems to me to be worth it to make friends with the Israelis sitting near you.

Hire an Israeli Singer

Looking for someone to play at a local celebration? Why not hire an Israeli singer or musician? Then, if you like him or her, invite them out for a coffee.

Importing Israelis

Another way to meet Israelis outside of Israel is to go out of our way to find some interesting Israelis – and invite them to our communities. Whether it's a business leader (and there are increasingly many of these who are Israeli), a writer, actor, singer, politician, judge, or professor, there are many Israelis who are interesting enough that it's worth springing for the price of a round trip ticket from Tel Aviv. Contact an Israeli organization directly (for example, universities for professors, political parties for politicians, publishers for authors, etc.) and mention your interest. A free ticket and some home hospitality for the guest when he or she arrives might just be enough. Throw in an invitation to some exclusive event happening locally and you might just end up fending them off with a stick.

Incidentally, inviting Israeli leaders in your profession or business to meet local leaders is, of course, also a great way of helping those Israelis and their companies increase business while showing off to your colleagues how worldly and cosmopolitan you really are (don't forget to smile here).

Finally, if you're looking for a place to start to find Israeli speakers, I'd suggest the nearest Israeli consulate or embassy – as most of them have a speakers bureau.

THINGS YOU CAN DO TODAY:

1. Eat at an Israeli restaurant. Make friends with the owner or the customer nearest you.
2. Go online and look for organizations, websites, and chat rooms where Israelis hang out.
3. Invite an Israeli to your home or to your business.
4. Hire an Israeli singer to play in a local band.
5. Take a class at the local college where the professor is an Israeli.
6. Go to Israeli movies and film festivals and make friends with the Israelis sitting near you.
7. Go to a synagogue and ask a few people if there are any new Israelis around to invite for a meal.
8. Sign up for a Hebrew class and get to know the Israeli teacher.
9. Ask the Israeli consulate nearest you for interesting Israeli speakers.
10. Think about paying for an Israeli leader to visit your community. Approach organizations directly with an offer.

5. Traveling to Israel

The man with the Uzi slung across his shoulder headed for the bank in downtown Jerusalem and shoved the glass doors open with a temper. Inside, he demanded money, his voice rising even as a manager came up to see what the hollering was about. Scarcely a moment later the threats began – delivered by the size-zero manager, an angry scowl appearing under her glasses. "You can't keep barging in here, Moshe," the woman berated the man, "we discussed all of this yesterday." A few moments later, the man with the Uzi slunk out of the bank, defeated, and I couldn't help but think: only in Israel.

Everyone ought to experience Israel at least once. It's a country full of so many wonderful contradictions that even just a short visit is likely to change your life for the better. I also can't think of a better way to help cement any bond you have with the country and turn you or any of the friends (or strangers) that you can convince to go into a lifelong advocate for its continued survival.

Did You Know?

The tourism industry in Israel employs close to 100,000 people, and brings in over $3 billion per year.

Mind you, I'm not saying that you won't find things (especially political issues) that may upset you when you arrive. But so what? At stake here is the country's continued existence. If you find things you want to change – welcome to Israel, a living

country, ever-changing. And if you just want to enjoy your trip –
welcome to Israel, a country that can promise you a truly unique
experience.

I. SHORT VISITS

Plan a Vacation

With Israel being in the news most often as a war-zone, it isn't
always obvious that it's still a great get-away spot for a vacation.
But even if you don't think about Holy spots, hiking or history –
Israel has some really great beaches, plenty of sun year-round
and lots of hotels, hot springs and spas eager to cater to you.
And no, you don't have to know Hebrew to enjoy it or to be safe.

It's also close to Europe, a cruise away from Greece and Turkey
and a natural stop on the way to the Far East. And I haven't even
mentioned romantic possibilities...

So here's what I suggest: Book a trip to Israel, even if it's a year
or two away. Plan it in your mind – and then tell a friend or your
family (thereby making it more real). Start a special account (in
the bank, or under the mattress) and label it the "Israel trip
money" – and then put in a few dollars each week. Depending
on where you live and how much you dedicate, within a
couple of years you'll probably have saved enough for at
least the airfare.

Join (or Plan) a Delegation

Whether you're a lawyer, judge, doctor, dentist, accountant,
engineer, politician, journalist, investor, scientist, banker, teacher
or even athlete, there's a delegation to Israel out there that you
will surely find interesting. And, in the unlikely event that you
can't find one, then contact a Jewish or Israeli organization and
start one!

Delegations to Israel are typically short visits that not only tour
the country's usual tourist traps but also hook you up with

people who work in and even lead the industries that are closest to yours in Israel.

Interaction with Israelis, a chance to make professional and business contacts and a nice vacation all wrapped into a single trip. Sign me up!

Religious or Political Missions

Quick – what country has enormous significance to three major religions and is at the heart of all-too-many front page headlines?

If you're at all interested in religion or politics then visiting Israel ought to be on the top of your traveling agenda. Not to put too fine a point on it, but if you haven't walked the streets of **Jerusalem** then you are missing out on some key understandings of Judaism, Christianity, Islam and all things related to the conflicts raging in the Middle East. Jerusalem is many things to many people, but it is an absolute must (in this author's humble opinion) to experience if you want to get a feel for the communities living in the region (Jerusalem has Arabs, Jews, Christians, Muslims, Armenians, and atheists – all in both the rich and poor variety), the confines of limited space and geography of the conflicts (Jerusalem's Old City is tiny and mountains dominate neighborhoods), and the paradoxes of the Middle East (Jerusalem has no physical boundary between Jewish and Arab neighborhoods, for instance, while minutes away a long security fence is the norm).

The latest leg in my long journey to the heart of Israel, which began when I first came here as a religious pilgrim over twenty years ago. For a very short period of time I was the only American president to visit Israel twice, then I became the only American president to visit Israel three times, and then four times.
President Bill Clinton

The options for combining a religious or political experience with a vacation are numerous. One can sign up for specifically Christian tours, for instance, which will highlight the **Via Dolorosa**, the **Garden of Gethsemane**, **Golgatha** and the **Church of the Holy Sepulchre** and still have fun dipping in the **Sea of Galilee** on the way to **Nazareth**. Or one can arrange to meet many of Israel's political or human rights leaders (who are often willing to say a few words to visiting groups in Jerusalem), take a helicopter tour to get a real feel for the country's size and beauty and spend a relaxing day at the beach – all within a few days.

Of course, conventional religion and politics are just the tip of the iceberg in Israel. Israel has plenty of opportunities for visitors to volunteer to be activists when it comes to helping the poor, fighting for the environment or just witnessing the fascinating melting pot of European, Russian, Ethiopian, Yemenite, Indian and other Jews.

Walk Forth on the Land

Whether you're an armchair military general interested in the strategic use of topography that helped Israel in the Yom Kippur War, or an avid backpacker who relishes climbing mountains and diving into waterfalls, you'll find plenty to attract you to Israel, while you leave your more timid friends and family members in the hotel. From giant craters in the **Negev** to swampland in the **Galilee**, and stopping off at the mountain peak of **Masada** in between, there are just plenty of reasons to make the trip, if you're at all the active type.

And if you're interested in history – don't forget to schedule a day or a week at one of Israel's many archaeological digs, while you're at it.

Join Some Older Folk

If you're on the other side of the retirement calendar, then consider making a trip to Israel with tours dedicated to retirees. Who needs to climb **Masada**? Grab a ride in the cable car to the top and enjoy smirking at the youngsters panting up the snake path. And why not have a day of study? Israel is the land where the Mishna (a collection of oral traditions that is the basis of the Talmud) was codified and is the home of probably the most yeshivas (schools for Talmudic study) per square foot. Or perhaps consider finding a few museums that are unique to the country and spending the day learning something you'll forget later as you relax to the sounds of the **Israeli Symphony** at night.

The country may be young, but there's plenty to entice people with some more experience behind them.

II. LONGER STAYS

Student Programs

I heartily recommend, to anyone young enough to consider it, a stay of at least one semester in Israel.

Whether it's a religious academy such as a yeshiva or seminary, or a university with an exchange program, there's just no better way to get to know the country and truly get a feel for what it means to live there than to be in the country for an extended period – and be in an institution geared towards teaching you not just whatever is on the curriculum but also an appreciation of the land and its peoples.

This is a win-win for anyone with an interest in traveling. There are plenty of languages spoken in Israel – just choose the friends you want to bond with! If you know of anyone who's thinking of a foreign experience, without losing a year, Israel should be a real consideration.

Did You Know?
The city of Eilat holds an international jazz festival every year.

Join a Kibbutz

For the socialists amongst us, or for those who just want a place to stay with free room and board for an extended time – consider finding a friendly kibbutz to join for a few months or a year. You'll work the land, pick fruit, clean garbage – and learn Hebrew, forge bonds with real Israelis and see the whole country from a unique perspective.

Enroll in a Hebrew Course (Ulpan)

Always felt that you ought to know Hebrew better? Or would really like to study the Bible in its original language? What better place to learn Hebrew than in the land where Hebrew is the vernacular? You can sign up for leisurely part-time courses, taught at Israeli universities, or a full-blown Ulpan (intensive course) that can be found either at universities or at private institutions (see, as usual, the resources list at the back of the book).

National Service and/or Army Service

Feeling patriotic? It's well known that Israelis are drafted at the age of 18 – men and women, both. Meanwhile, people who love Israel, visit regularly and enjoy its benefits – but who are not Israeli residents – don't have any such obligation. If that doesn't seem quite cricket to you – well, here's your chance to balance the books a bit, by volunteering.

You can go all out and volunteer to serve in the **IDF** (whether for 3 weeks, 3 months or 3 years – the army has many options) or you can contact the folks who coordinate national service programs, which began primarily as an alternative to military service for Orthodox women. Examples of such national service can include working with the disabled, educating children in impoverished Israeli towns, and working with the unemployed. This is Israel's local version of the Peace Corps and well worth considering if you want to both help the country and have an enriching experience that will look great on a resumé. Contact **www.sherut-leumi.co.il**, **www.aminadav.org.il**, or **www.bat-ami.org.il** for more details.

III. MOVING TO ISRAEL

No guide for helping Israel could possibly be complete without mentioning that life-changing possibility of actually moving to the country. Bringing all your amazing energy, resources and enthusiasm to the country itself is surely the best way of helping the country grow and be strong for decades to come.

Fortunately, if you are interested in this adventure, there are many people who have paved the way and can help out with logistics, cultural adaptation, and general changes you almost certainly will encounter. Some of the best organizations to contact include **AACI**, **Nefesh b'Nefesh**, and **Tehilla** (see the resources list at the back of the book for details).

THINGS YOU CAN DO TODAY:

1. Book a trip to Israel – even if it's a year away.
2. Start a special account or just a place under your favorite mattress and put some money in it every week to use towards your trip.
3. Find out about any local professionals, investors, athletes, businesspeople or other groups of people who are planning a trip – and sign up.
4. Decide to visit some Holy sites of the three major Western religions – plan a trip by yourself or with your local spiritual leader(s).
5. Contact political parties in Israel and ask about arranging leaders to meet a group of tourists – and then find some people to go with you on a trip.
6. Think about sponsoring local leaders to come with you on your trip to Israel.
7. Schedule a day or longer at an archaeological dig in Israel, and get your hands dirty with history.
8. Research programs available through your college (or your kid's college) to do some learning abroad. A summer, semester, or a year in Israel can be life-changing.

9. Volunteer on a Kibbutz – it's a great experience for a small amount of expense.
10. Sign up for a Hebrew course in Israel – what better place to study Hebrew?
11. Research possibilities within National or Military Services in Israel (talk to your local consulate to start). There are programs as short as 3 weeks.
12. Plan a pilot trip to Israel and consider the possibility of making it your permanent home.
13. Run an Israel-related contest and offer a free trip as the prize. If such a contest already exists in your area – enter it!

6. Improving Relations between Jews and Non-Jews

A priest and a rabbi walk into a bar – okay, you've heard this joke before. But here's something you may not have thought about: the very fact that a joke can assume that a priest and a rabbi are friendly enough to go out and get sloshed together. Now, that's progress (historically speaking).

You may not be a priest or a rabbi, but, believe it or not, tossing down a few Jack Daniels with a member of another faith can be your own small contribution to Israel's survival. How's that, you say? Well, the fact is that the State of Israel and the Jewish people are heavily interconnected (despite those who may be unhappy about this) and that means that every Jew is an ambassador of sorts, whether they like it or not (and, yes, that includes those Jews who think they have nothing to do with Israel). With the Jewish people and Israel so closely identified with each other in public opinion, it only makes sense that one of the easiest ways to help Israel is to foster good relations between Jews and non-Jews around the world.

In addition, every non-Jew has the potential to not only enrich their own existence by befriending Jews but they also have the opportunity to help Israel in a uniquely non-political way. Each act of friendly relations between Jews and non-Jews indirectly affects the tolerance of the cultures where we live as well as the

Jewish State itself. This is truly one of the easiest and most local ways of contributing.

One word of caution, though, when it comes to socializing with members of other faiths: Remember that each group takes its faith seriously. I'm in no way suggesting that Jews or Christians should try to convert the other into sharing their religious beliefs.

Start by Smiling

I'm a big believer in the power of a simple smile. Whether it's to your neighbor's bratty child or to the boss who deserves to sink to the lowest rungs of Hell, a smile has the power to change another person's very pattern of thought. It can open up a line of communication that never existed before, or brighten a person's day, despite hardship. It is, in short, a powerful weapon – and we should use it to help us interact with people of other faiths and races.

When in doubt, smile.

Make Friends at Work

You see these people all the time, you work in the same building or even the same company, you hold meetings with them and exchange e-mails and phone messages, but you have no idea what their spouse's name is. Does that sound familiar? This is the easiest – and hardest – place to make new friends. But if you're interested in helping Israel and extending inter-faith relationships, work is the first place to start. You're talking to people anyway – why not ask a tentative personal question? Or make an exploratory comment about something in the news relating to Israel (something not overtly political, perhaps – like a new invention from an Israeli company, or a recent Israeli business deal. For ideas, check out **Globes**, Israel's main business news journal).

Hang Out Online

This is one of the easiest ways to "meet" people of different faiths and races. Do an internet search for Jewish, Christian, Moslem, Hindu and other groups and start visiting and hanging out on their blogs and websites. Not only will you get an education, but you will probably make some far-off friends too.

Utilize Community Centers

Many cities and small towns have community centers that are open to everyone. Even if you don't want to use their gym or pool, they often have educational classes. You can simply join a class and befriend strangers.

Join a Book Club

A city-wide or neighborhood book club is a great way to get to know strangers on an ongoing basis and exchange ideas as well as favorite books. Try to find one with people you don't already know.

Go Dancing

Take a class in Israeli dancing – what better way to meet Jews and have fun? If you're Jewish, take a class in salsa or, better yet, in Indian *gorba* dancing.

Read Their Newspapers

Many communities have their own local and national newspapers. Just by reading the Jewish ones, for example, you'll have a much better idea of what Jews in your city are thinking about, and where they're going for fun activities.

Share Your Emotions

The heart is a powerful bonding tool. If Jews and non-Jews share their desires, grief and emotional experiences, it will bond them together. This is true for individuals you are becoming friendly with (it's all too tempting to keep those budding friendships superficial – don't do it; share your joys and pain) and for whole communities (having a memorial ceremony on **Holocaust Day**, for instance).

Shop at an Ethnic Store

Try some new food, patronize a member of another ethnic group and potentially make new friends – all by shopping at each other's stores. And while you're there, don't be afraid to ask about customs or practices you were always curious about. If you don't ask, you won't find out.

Ask Questions about Other Religions

If you've always been the curious type, visit a place of worship or a school of another faith – and ask a few basic questions about that faith. Or start by chatting online. Be careful that you don't step over any lines, though, and avoid people trying to convert you unless you're looking for conversion.

Take a Course

Whether it's at the community center or continuing education or even at the local synagogue, church or mosque, learning about each other's religious beliefs is a good way to understand each other as well as making some good contacts.

Play Sports

Sports is a great way to be active together, have a sense of team-work and get to know people in a neutral politics-free zone. Find a sport that you like (or at least don't hate) and join a league outside of your religious community.

Enroll Your Tots in Mixed Playgroups

When they're so young it doesn't matter where they go, make a point of taking them somewhere where you'll meet parents that are unlike you.

Check Out Local Jewish Sites When Traveling

If you're traveling almost anywhere in the world, take an afternoon to go off the beaten track and hunt up some local Jewish sites. When in Europe, especially, these can be hidden gems, offering rare historical insight to the local region and will also afford you the opportunity to meet some local Jews.

On the flip side, if your local synagogue or Jewish museum is likely to be an interesting attraction to visitors, don't forget to advertise that fact in places where tourists are likely to come across it.

Invite Speakers of Other Faiths

Invite people of other faiths who have interesting life stories to speak at events and at schools. You can find such people by reading feature stories in local papers or online. Or calling a local paper and speaking to a reporter who covers the local beat.

Commemorate Holocaust Day

Have a memorial on **Holocaust Day**, even if there are few Jews in your town (it's a good reason to invite some, too). Everyone can learn something from this tragedy.

Work with Other Generations

If you're young, volunteer at an old age home; if you have a few more years under your belt, offer to mentor a student. If you keep your eyes open there will be great opportunities to meet people of different faiths and to forge genuine bonds while working together.

Contact Authors

Here's an interesting way to make a new acquaintance: Read a book about another faith and write a letter to the author.

IMPROVING RELATIONS BETWEEN JEWS AND NON-JEWS

Have a "Clean Up Day"

Do a "Clean Up Day" with your friends or family and pick up
litter from the neighborhood, while trying to get other locals
involved. If you advertise ahead of time, you may actually get
other people willing to help.

Teach a Class

If you're feeling proactive, then offer to teach a class about
your faith, specifically in a non-preachy way. Many Jews would
be interested in a "Fundamentals of..." for other religions,
for example.

Have a Street Party

Whether you arrange an outdoor flea market, open to the public,
or whether you just knock on everyone's door and invite them to
your living room for some cake and coffee, it's a great idea to
get to know your neighbors. And maybe some of your neighbors' friends too. If you're feeling like this is a bit weird, then try
tying it to an external event or holiday, whether it's a sports
event or **Labor Day**. If it's good weather, consider including a
barbeque. A word of caution: remember that Jews who eat only
kosher food will probably make do with just a soda or the equivalent. If you tell people up front that they don't have to feel
uncomfortable not eating, that will probably help.

Learn a Foreign Language

Study Hebrew to meet Jews, study almost any other language
to meet everyone else. This is a particularly good idea for Jews
living close to communities where a foreign language is widely
spoken, such as Spanish in New York City. Start by learning one
new word each week. Or enroll in a formal course.

Involve Your Kids

There are inter-faith programs that are geared to children. Some
of them are just fun activities, without any inter-faith programming. Others try to teach tolerance by having kids share stories

of their homes and growing up in different cultures, or by more creative ideas such as making clay pizzas (each "slice" representing another community), or having the kids draw face masks of other kids from different races.

Get Active Locally

Join the PTA, run for City Council, volunteer at an animal shelter, offer to tutor your neighbor's kids, take an emergency first aid course – do something that will force you to interact with strangers and therefore give them the opportunity to get to know you. If you're Jewish, then by definition you're helping Israel just by being a friendly person to all the non-Jews you're sure to meet. If you're not Jewish, then keep your eyes open for the Jews you are likely to meet – and extend them a smile. If you're really brave, invite some strangers to join you for a coffee.

Find Common Causes

Whether it's a local issue, a national political issue or a charitable fundraiser, getting involved in causes will give you the opportunity to meet new people – Jews and non-Jews alike. No matter what side of any issue you're on, you're almost guaranteed to find some Jews working on it.

Go to a Town Meeting

There's nothing like discussing our shared future to realize that there are good reasons to get along. Try attending a forum where your city's future is being discussed. If there are Jews living in your city, there should be an opportunity to have some real discussions.

Throw a Cross-cultural Weekend

Why should only businesses have fancy retreats? Rent a hotel for the weekend and invite the world. Or, if you're feeling even more active, try renting a camp or army base for the weekend and plan a busy program, dividing the days between outdoor activities and socializing with a few lectures throw in.

*We support poor Gentiles with the poor people of
Israel, and we visit sick Gentiles as well as the sick of
Israel and we bury the dead of the Gentiles as well as
the dead of Israel, because of the ways of peace.*
The Talmud; Gitin 61a

Take Advantage of College Life

Taking advantage of college ought to also mean meeting people
outside of your comfort zone, and it's often the first opportunity
for Jews and non-Jews to get to know each other as people and
not just stereotypes.

So, in addition to any pro-Israel activities on campus that are
worthwhile to either start or partake in (see the chapter **Helping
Israel on Campus: The College Years**), it's worth organizing
events that reach out to Jews and non-Jews alike that don't
overtly involve Israel.

Open fun events to any student on campus – and then mingle.
Have a paintball day or a trip to a local amusement park.
Arrange for students to feed the homeless at a soup kitchen.
Have an open party at a nearby pub or club. Organize a sports
week, either on campus or off.

For events that are clearly labeled as "inter-faith", you might
want to consider a "religion week," where each faith holds
lectures, events, dances and the like for one day of the week
on your campus. Then make sure that you check out the other
faith's programs.

Other inter-faith ideas can include college radio shows that
feature religious debate, running programs for clerical students
(any kind of program, as long as they partake jointly), joining an
inter-faith organization, and having inter-faith debates on or off
campus (hiring speakers, for instance, and then having drinks).

In addition, it's worth getting the Jewish students' unions and organizations to sponsor or run joint events with other unions and organizations. A great way to meet each other and to talk about all kinds of topics, Israel-related and other.

Of course, the easiest way of meeting each other is to simply take classes together and to join student organizations and to be friendly.

Twin Schools

Have a Jewish and non-Jewish school sports league or combined courses on citizenship and tolerance. Even limited involvement with each other can lead children to remember that we all look the same under our skins. Better yet, invite a few Israeli kids to join too.

THINGS YOU CAN DO TODAY:

1. Remember that you are an ambassador for your faith. When Jews and non-Jews are friendly to each other, Israel benefits.
2. Smile at a stranger.
3. Visit a place of worship or a school that is from another faith – and ask a few basic questions about that faith.
4. Look for people of other faiths online.
5. Look for people of other faiths at work, and talk about things not related to work.
6. Read a Jewish newspaper or magazine (if you're Jewish, read a different newspaper or magazine).
7. Shop at an ethnic store.
8. Join an inter-faith organization (online or off).
9. Take a class in Israeli dancing. If you're Jewish, take a class in a different kind of dancing.
10. Put your kids in a common playgroup or sports league (and then be sure to talk to the other parents too).
11. Join a sports league; or at least go to some games and cheer.
12. Read a book about another faith and write a letter to the author.
13. Check out local Jewish sites, at home and when traveling.

14. Volunteer at a soup kitchen.
15. Invite people of other faiths who have interesting life stories to speak at events and at schools. You can find such people by reading feature stories in local papers.
16. Spend some time at an old age home, and ask people about their lives and what they think is important.
17. Join things and invite strangers for a coffee. Good examples are the PTA, book clubs, charities, and environmental movements.
18. Have a street party, or a building party, with or without a BBQ.
19. Organize a paintball day and make it an open invitation.
20. Have a "religion week" on a local campus, where each day another religion holds events and invites speakers.
21. Have a "kids interfaith" event at a community center or local gym.
22. Go on spring break (or another vacation) to a place that needs help with disaster relief, and volunteer – possibly the simplest way a Jew can be certain of making a friend for life within the non-Jewish world.
23. Do a "Clean Up Day" with friends or family and pick up litter from the neighborhood, while trying to get other locals involved.
24. Get involved in causes – political or apolitical.
25. Offer to mentor a student in your area of expertise. Post the offer in a place where people not like you will see it.
26. Have a memorial on **Holocaust Day**, even if there are few Jews in your town (it's a good reason to invite some, too).
27. Teach a course about your faith at the local community center.
28. Arrange a cross-cultural weekend retreat, with fun activities along with speakers on topics interesting to many religions.
29. Learn a foreign language – enroll in a course.
30. Twin your school to a local Jewish school.

PART 3

AT WORK AND
AS COMMUNITIES

7. Creating Business Ties and Trade with Israelis

In the "good old" (i.e. bad old) days before the hi-tech revolution, I might have labeled this chapter "Teach an Israeli to Fish."

But the patronizing days when foreigners presumed to guide Israeli businesses (teaching them to fish) and then purchase their products went the way of the horse-and-buggy the moment that Israeli hi-tech companies like **ICQ** sold themselves to foreigners for "bargains" at over $100 million. In any case, today it ought to suffice to say that Israeli companies are no longer charity cases. Indeed, today's Israeli company competing for attention on the world stage is generally top-of-the-line.

In fact, Israel as a whole is doing financially better than it ever has. Its per-capita income is at all-time highs, it is borrowing less money from the world than it is lending, its public debt is at record lows and its standing as a world leading center for technology and innovation is heralded as a matter of course by top business leaders the world over.

Which ought to make the notion of creating or strengthening business ties with Israelis very attractive.

And, oh yeah – it's one of the absolute best ways to help Israel. Which ought to go without saying, considering that by buying from, trading with, or investing in Israeli companies we directly help their Israeli employees and their families and indirectly help the whole country improve its financial standing.

Israel has amazing people. We are investing
$4 billion in an amazing group of people from Israel –
and we are investing it at an astounding speed.
Warren Buffet, Chairman and CEO of Berkshire
Hathaway, May 2006

Buy Israeli

So how do we get started? Well, first we have to decide that we're not just giving charity when we buy Israeli. Giving charity is great, but it will never represent but a portion of where our income or revenue goes – and especially our business revenue.

So here's a reasonable decision, I think, for us to take: Assuming that all other things are basically equal, we should choose an Israeli product or service, at least some of the time, whether for our personal lives or for business solutions.

A Few Numbers and Facts:

- *Total Israeli Exports in 1950: $18 million. Exports in 2005: $36.6 billion.*
- *Israel's 2006 national debt ratio fell to only 86% of the GDP – the lowest rate in Israel's history.*
- *Israel has the 6th largest number of biotechnology companies, with 139 operating at the end of 2006. From mid 2005 to the end of 2006, Israeli biotechnology companies raised over $127 million in IPO's on the TASE.*
- *2007: Decision made to allow Israel to become a member of the OECD, The Organization for Economic Co-Operation and Development, a group of 30 developed countries committed to democracy and the market economy.*

Once we've decided to buy Israeli (at least sometimes), the trick is to find Israeli products or services. Sometimes this is as easy as going to a local supermarket or pharmacy and looking for Israeli names (see the box in this chapter for a small sampling of famous Israeli brands), but the best way by far is to go online and spend about two minutes searching. A quick search of "Israeli products" or adding "Israel" to your search for, say, chocolates or digital security, will come up with lots of ideas. And if you want a few quick sites to check out, I'd suggest hopping over to **www.shopinisrael.com, www.export.org.il, www.israeliproducts.com, http://middleeastfacts.com/mef_buy-israeli-products.php** or **http://www.ou.org/programs/5762/buyisrael.htm.**

Spend Ten Dollars

It's important, I believe, to make a decision to buy at least a set amount of Israeli products each month. This makes it part of our routines. So, for example, setting aside just $10 at the beginning of each month and dedicating it for Israeli goods can get us into the habit of buying a few Israeli chocolate bars, cosmetics or candles on a regular basis. Small amounts, by the way, add up quickly and are significant. Israel's whole economy, even while doing better than ever before, is still tiny. Total exports are measured in the tens of billions of dollars – and if each household bought only a few extra Israeli exports, the numbers would have a direct positive impact.

Spread the Word about Israeli Products

Tell your friends and coworkers about Israeli products or services that you like. This doesn't have to be preachy – you can eat a chocolate bar in front of them or apply a Dead Sea hand cream in the company washroom.

Give Israeli Products as Gifts

You might also want to offer Israeli products to your co-workers, customers and clients – as gifts. This is an especially good idea during holiday season, when gifts are customary. Not to mention being a good idea for promotions to customers or to butter up the boss on his or her birthday. It isn't pushy or proselytizing to send someone Israeli chocolate or cosmetics.

Israel's Main Exports:

- Agro-technology
- Aviation and Aerospace
- Electronics
- Fashion and Textiles
- Jewelry, Arts and Crafts
- Life Science Technologies
- Software

- Automotive Technology
- Cosmetics and Toiletries
- Environmental Items
- Food and Beverages
- Judaica
- Security and Safety
- Telecommunications

Tell Your Clients about Israel

Send your clients and customers information about industry-related news and events in Israel. This carries inherent interest while advertising Israel in a positive way. Read **Globes** for breaking business news.

Add an Israeli Website Link

Suggest to whoever is in charge of the company website to add Israeli website links (that are relevant and appropriate, obviously). And ask those Israeli sites to do the same. A couple of e-mails is all this should take.

Sell to Israelis

The flip side of buying is selling, and there's no reason that you can't sell your own wares to Israelis if they're at all interested in buying. Assuming that you're not peddling snake oil, selling needed services or products to Israeli companies can help those companies with their own bottom line, while improving your ties and relationships to Israel (not to mention your bottom line). It's also a great way for Israel to accumulate allies in the business world (and therefore in the political world) – after all, what better incentive for a major company to lobby for Israel than the fact that Israeli companies are their clients?

Hire Israelis

Here's a thought: how about recruiting among Israelis? Most Israelis are at least bilingual (English, Russian and French are common second languages in Israel) and the country is small enough that when you hire a few Israelis you have connections with half the Israeli world in your industry.

> *Israel has a clear comparative advantage in knowledge-based information-technology – products and services.*
> **Moody's Investors Services**

You can hire a full time employee, grab an intern from an Israeli university for a late summer internship (their year ends later than most) or go all-out and open an Israeli branch (however large or small) of your company. Then again, your best bet might be to simply out-source to an Israeli company or contractor. Stay at home, get the benefit of Israeli know-how and pay in your own currency. Sounds good to me!

Invest in Israeli Securities

Israeli companies listed on NASDAQ, AIM and other world markets, mutual funds specializing in Israel, Venture Capital funds focusing on Israeli start-ups, Israeli bonds – there are a plethora of ways for you or your company to park at least some long-term cash and pension funds in a way that will both make good financial sense and help Israel.

> *Israel has transformed from a country that borrows money from the world, into a country that lends it.*
> **Serhan Cevik, Morgan Stanley's Vice President for Middle East and North Africa.**

Talk to your company's financial advisor(s) and pension fund managers and brainstorm. At the very least, consider investing in Israeli blue-chips like **Teva** or **Checkpoint**.

Take Advantage of Special Benefits

There are sometimes grants, tax benefits or other advantages to conducting business in Israel or with Israelis. For example, Israel has **Free Trade Agreements** with the United States, Canada, Mexico, and with much of Europe, providing opportunities to export via Israel. There are often government sponsored programs that will encourage businesses to invest in R&D factories in special areas of Israel and a number of Israeli cities "twin" with other cities worldwide, giving those cities access to Israeli contacts that others, in other cities, won't find as easily. Call your nearest Israeli consulate or go online and do some research – it could pay off in a real way.

Suggest Israel-related Charities to Support

If it so happens that your company is looking for a tax deductible charity to donate funds to, consider suggesting an apolitical Israel-related one. Any of the "Friends of" charities, such as **Friends of the Hebrew University of Jerusalem (www.afhu.org**, for the **American Friends organization**) or the **American Society for the Protection of Nature in Israel (www.aspni.org**) ought to be appropriate, considering that they are merely Israeli versions of causes your company is probably used to supporting – that is, education and the environment.

Top 10 Ways to Help Israel at Work:

1. **Put a picture of Israel on your desk or wall. Or hang a calendar.**
2. **Invite an Israeli businessperson to give a seminar.**
3. **Check out Israeli companies on the internet for business solutions.**
4. **Network with Israeli businesspeople.**
5. **Order lunch from an Israeli restaurant.**
6. **Bring an Israeli product to work (even a chocolate bar or face-wash will do).**
7. **Buy a co-worker an Israeli gift.**
8. **Throw an Israeli wine and cheese bash.**

9. Offer a trip to Israel as a holiday bonus.
10. Charge a small amount for a "silly costume" day and donate the funds to an Israeli charity.

Notice Where Israel is Heading

Israel is making a conscious effort to become the premier R&D center for the world's knowledge economy. In the energy sector it is planning to turn the Negev into a research center for alternative sources of energy (especially solar); in the biotech industry, Israeli companies specialize in genetic R&D, diagnosis, drug delivery and stem cell and tissue engineering; in software, computers and electronics Israel is continually making innovations, particularly in security and nano-technology; and, of course, Israel continues to innovate in the military technology sphere.

> *For Microsoft, having an R&D center in Israel has been a great experience.*
> **Bill Gates**

Keeping abreast of Israeli research should be a must for any company that hopes to take competitive advantage of new technologies. Reading Israeli newspapers (online or in print) and browsing Israeli scientific journals are good ideas for any business today. To start, check out the Israeli business paper **Globes** as well as the more famous general papers such as the **Jerusalem Post** or **Haaretz**. Pay a visit to the Israeli foreign ministry's website too (**www.mfa.gov.il**), and click on its "beyond politics" link. You may be surprised by the sheer number of deals Israeli companies are involved in.

In short, strengthening business ties to Israel is something that one day may be a necessity for all businesses – and we, as people who care about Israel, should help speed that day along.

Buy Israeli Technology

While we're talking about Israeli technology, if your company is looking for a hi-tech solution to a problem, or you just want to think about how to improve your existing business by importing some hi-tech ideas, I'd bet dollars to donuts that there's an Israeli company who can help. Start by searching online, and if that doesn't work, then call up the nearest Israeli consulate and ask.

Meet Israeli Businesspeople

Hands down the best way to know what's going on in the world of Israeli business and check out for yourself whether there's an opportunity worth exploring is to meet Israeli businesspeople in the flesh and talk to them. Network with them, schmooze, and encourage them to talk to your boss or colleagues.

But how do you find Israelis, you might wonder? Well, the easiest way is to invite them! Most Israelis know that that their businesses rely on exports and they'll be more than happy to join organizations, speak at local Chambers of Commerce or industry conferences, present at exhibitions or just come by your office for a chat. Start by asking people you know if they know of anyone, expand your search through the internet, talk to the Israeli consulate and Chamber of Commerce and write to the heads of Israeli companies. It's often surprising how easygoing and accessible Israelis can be.

Plan a Company Trip to Israel

Why search locally for Israelis when there's a whole country of 'em sitting in Israel? There are international conferences held in Tel Aviv and Jerusalem – and if there isn't one in your field, then that could be your opportunity to start one.

Israel could be a great place to mix business with pleasure – think Eilat as a vacation spot for favored employees with a side trip to Tel Aviv for business. Or go for a real estate investment by buying a company apartment in the Holy Land and send your workers there as a holiday bonus.

And if you want to strengthen your ties with other non-Israeli companies or professionals while still supporting Israel (and maybe learning a thing or two on the way), consider planning or joining a delegation of industry professionals on a trip to Israel. There are trips like these planned by Jewish and Christian organizations – and if you can't find one already in existence, then carpe that diem and plan one yourself!

Some Famous Israeli Brand Names:

Achva (Halva)
Ahava (Skin Care)
Beigle & Beigle (Pretzels and Crackers)
Carmel (Beverages)
Elite (Chocolate, Candy)
Golan (Beverages)
Gottex (Swimwear)
Kvuzat Yavne (Pickles, Olives)
Naot (Sandals)
Osem (Grocery Food)
Sabra (Salads)
Telma (Grocery Food)
Tnuva (Cheese)
Wissotzky (Tea)

THINGS YOU CAN DO TODAY:

1. Buy Israeli. Decide to buy at least $10 worth of Israeli products each month.
2. Tell your friends and coworkers about Israeli products or services that you like.
3. Read an Israeli newspaper (online or off), such as **Jerusalem Post**, **Haaretz**, **Yediot** or **Globes**. Distribute them to coworkers in your office.
4. Browse through an Israeli scientific journal. Check out the websites of major Israeli universities (**Hebrew University**, **Technion**, **Weizman Institute**).
5. Send your clients and customers information about industry-related news and events in Israel. A useful place for articles is **www.israel21c.org**.

6. Offer Israeli products to your customers and clients – either selling those products or giving them as gifts, especially around the holidays and birthdays.
7. Put Israeli website links on your company's website.
8. Ask your suppliers and retailers if they stock Israeli products. If they don't, suggest a few. (Same goes for your local supermarket).
9. Invest in Israeli securities and/or bonds. Discuss this with your financial advisor(s) and/or the managers of the company pension funds.
10. Sell your products or services to an Israeli company.
11. Network with Israeli businesspeople. Invite Israelis to speak at conferences, at networking events, at professional associations or to your employees and/or coworkers at your office. Recruit Israeli companies to exhibit at trade shows. Ask Israeli companies to join when there's a network of companies meeting in your industry.
12. Ask an Israeli to teach a mini-course to your employees. This can be a course about how things work in Israel, or even a Hebrew language course.
13. Call the nearest Israeli consulate or the Israeli Chamber of Commerce and ask to meet with visiting Israelis who are in your industry.
14. Hire an Israeli. This can be by outsourcing or by finding an intern or employee.
15. Use Israeli models in your advertisements (another take on hiring Israelis).
16. Invite Israeli companies to bid on your projects.
17. Check out Israeli companies on the internet for business solutions. If your company needs something that involves technology in any way, chances are there's an Israeli out there willing to provide it, hopefully with a competitive spirit.
18. Send employees to Israel to network.
19. Offer a trip to Israel as a holiday bonus.
20. Lead a delegation of executives or other professionals to Israel.
21. Think about investing in Israeli real estate.
22. Consider the idea of opening an R&D branch in Israel.

8. Creating Organizational and Community Ties to Israeli Organizations and Communities

As individuals, we have the power to change the world. But as groups of individuals – organized into companies and communities – our power is exponentially greater. But of course we know that already. We are already joined to communities, cities, companies and organizations in our regular lives. Whether we join these as willingly as a youngster volunteering for the Marines or as reluctantly as a lemming heading with his brothers for that cliff, we cannot help but be a part of groups larger than ourselves.

The purpose of this chapter, then, is to be a quick guide to some ways of taking these very organizations and communities that we belong to (including those that have little or no natural connection to Israel) and creating human, cultural, economic and organizational links to the organizations and communities of the Jewish State.

Twin Your City

Why don't we start with the cities (or towns or villages) that we inhabit? The concept of twinning a city, whereby two cities agree to share cultural and business links with each other, is a great

63

opportunity for anyone interested in helping Israel. There are already many such programs in place to easily emulate and both cities benefit.

Cities that are twinned will often send delegations of business leaders to each other's cities, share in cultural or educational activities, discuss common interests – be they global ones such as environmental concerns or local ones such as how each city conducts crime-fighting or treats sewage, run student exchange programs, and promote cooperation between their respective colleges and universities.

If your city does not already twin with a city in Israel, then this can be a great venture to push for. Lobby your local Chamber of Commerce and local politicians and investigate possibilities within Israel for cities or towns that have industries or people that you think your own townspeople might appreciate. For example, **Haifa** is a port city and has a large oil refinery – perhaps your own city is known for its port or oil connections. Or, on a smaller scale, there are kibbutzim with expertise on agriculture and water development that might have surprisingly much to teach a desert community or a rural farming community.

Of course, trade flows both ways. There are many cities outside of Israel that might view twinning as a great marketing entrée to Israeli hi-tech firms who can be both suppliers and customers.

And, as it happens, cities can and do twin with more than one city in more than one country. **New York**, for instance, has ten twins, including both **Jerusalem** and **Cairo**. (For a partial list of Israeli cities that are already twinned, check out **http://www.sistercities.org/icrc/directory/MiddleEast/Israel**).

Of course, if your city already twins with an Israeli one, then it should be all the easier to get involved and help with – or create – programs that benefit both communities. Some examples of programs you might want to suggest, if they aren't being pursued already, are ones that invite police and terrorism experts to visit each other, joint government or business conferences (or conferences that are held in each city in alternating years), ongoing student communications over secure internet connections in the classroom (New York and Jerusalem cooperate on one such, called the **Internet-based Educational Exchange** Program), joint art displays (perhaps alternating years, with museums cooperating or classes sending in their best students' work), teaching about the twin city in the classroom, and holding events in each city's main parks that display art or wares from the other city.

School Ties

Colleges are one of the most dynamic organizations in any city or community and if you belong to one then you should try to beef up any ties with Israel you can – whether it's a simple faculty exchange program, cooperation on joint projects in the arts or sciences, joint applications for research and development grants, or easing the way for students to receive credit for courses taken in Israel's universities.

On lower levels of education, summer camps that give discounts to Israeli children, schools that offer Hebrew as an option, and any willingness by the school to fund even a part of an educational trip to Israel, are all great ideas. For that matter, there's no reason why not to twin with an Israeli elementary or high school and do a faculty exchange (for a year, let's say) with teachers who may be willing or to conduct other joint programs. A good example of one such program is the **Jerusalem-New York Environmental Challenge**, supported by the **UJA-Federation** of New York and Israel's **Ministry of the Environment**, where a number of elementary schools in New York and Israel spend a month studying their own and one another's ecological footprint and environmental habits and work together to improve their local environment (for more information about this, check out **www.svivaisrael.org**).

Non Profit Bonds

Whether it's for the purpose of donating blood or helping to feed the needy, there's every reason for non profit organizations outside of Israel to communicate with Israeli non profits that are doing the same type of activities in Israel. If you work for or belong to a non profit – ask about their Israeli counterparts. Perhaps the organizations can help each other, whether by displaying links on their websites, selling each other's t-shirts, or giving gifts to donors for donating to both organizations at once. In addition, the professionals who work in these organizations ought to benefit from regular communication and conferences.

Incidentally, I would like to add a word about the value of formalizing contacts and support within and between organizations. By issuing joint declarations, running cooperative fundraising and linking the organizations' names in public, there is a value and level of relationship added that is not there when it is merely a couple of individuals who happen to work for their respective organizations in the two countries and who phone or e-mail each other occasionally. Each level of formal recognition for an Israeli non profit adds a subtle layer of recognition of Israel's very existence and legitimacy. This is certainly worth at least a small bureaucratic fight over.

Calendar Events

Does your community celebrate Israel's **Independence Day** at all? If not – how about suggesting it? You don't have to put on a parade (like New York) – even a small Israeli flag flying on city buildings or at public schools for the day would spark good conversations. Or some Israeli music played on local radio stations or a talk show host talking about it could be interesting.

Perhaps suggest a free day of an Israeli channel that day to your local cable or satellite TV provider, as a marketing gimmick for them – and some cultural communication for Israel.

Other calendar events can include **Holocaust Day** (not a direct Israeli reference, but it can, of course, tie in) and some mention of Israel on some of the Jewish holidays throughout the year.

Cultural Connections

Art, music, food, dance – many of us belong to or participate in events run by organizations dedicated to these very things. Why not suggest an expansion of their repertoire to include a few Israeli samples?

Whether it's a museum at which you're a member, a philharmonic that you espouse or a beer festival that you attend annually, there's almost always room for suggesting an Israeli component to the organizers for a future program.

> *Israel was not created in order to disappear –*
> *Israel will endure and flourish. It is the child*
> *of hope and the home of the brave. It can neither*
> *be broken by adversity nor demoralized by success.*
> *It carries the shield of democracy and it honors*
> *the sword of freedom.*
> **President John F. Kennedy**

For that matter, even on a micro scale, such as attending an art class or starting a band in your garage, why not share your experiences with Israelis doing the same thing? With online groups (such as **facebook**, among others) becoming "friends" with Israelis with similar interests is simple. And from such connections opportunities develop.

International Organizations

International organizations have become powerhouses in our day, whether they are organizations run by committees from various governments, all the many NGO's or informal, even ad-hoc, "organizations" that spring up for an event and disappear after the event is over. And it's no secret that many of these groups have agendas that are anti-Israel.

To be effective supporters of Israel's right to exist we need to belong to both the organizations that fight on behalf of Israel and to the ones which can all too easily be taken over by a vocal minority agitating against the Jewish State. This is especially true of organizations whose purpose is not Israel related at all.

67

A good example is the trade unions that were calling for a boycott of Israeli academic institutions – a great example of an organization that it is important to both join and be active in, even if only to be vocal against such proposals – and the groups that are dedicated to fighting for academic freedom and opposed to boycotting (such as the **Bar Ilan** University-based **International Advisory Board for Academic Freedom**).

I believe that whenever we have the opportunity to join a large (and especially international) organization, it's important to seize it as a way not to just benefit from the organization's meetings and contacts – but as a way of both monitoring its developments and influencing its direction. Once you're a member, many things are possible. For example, the simple act of inviting your Israeli friends and contacts to join the organization with you can imbue the group with a subtle pro-Israel flavor that will enhance the organization itself while simultaneously helping Israel. Similarly, suggesting to your new contacts at the organization links and connections to Israelis in their line of work can only be beneficial. Not to mention suggesting the possibility of starting an Israeli branch, if one doesn't already exist.

With governmental and quasi-governmental organizations this issue is even more important. If you belong to one it would be a smart move to get to know the movers and shakers personally, and perhaps introduce them to some Israeli culture, books, art, or films. Try to get a position on the organization's finance committee, on their newsletter or on their steering committee. Become a respected member whose opinions are sought after in general, so that when issues come up you are already a known commodity. In addition, try to expand or initiate links to Israeli government and quasi-government organizations. Even a simple mutual web link is a start. Perhaps suggest fact finding missions or commissioning reports that will include an Israeli facet that is relevant (for example on Israeli biotechnological solutions for oil spills, if you belong to a group with a mandate to be concerned about environmental dangers). Since there are Israeli companies developing almost every kind of technological solution possible for a wide range of problems, starting with researching Israeli hi-tech solutions would be a natural place to commission a study or mission.

> *Israel must never be expected to jeopardize her security: if she was ever foolish enough to do so, and then suffered for it, the backlash against both honest brokers and Palestinians would be immense.*
> **Margaret Thatcher**

Other possibilities can include facilitating the meeting of members from countries with no formal ties with Israel and Israelis. What better way to thaw out a cold peace (much less temper a hot war) than to foster communications between Israelis and their erstwhile enemies on subjects that are neutral? International organizations (especially those with conferences in Europe) are a natural venue for such informal links and meetings.

Similarly, third party "deals," in which companies from countries formally at war with Israel get to do business with Israeli companies by going through a neutral third country, are often possible to set up in the halls of conferences of international organizations – if you look out for the opportunity to introduce your Israeli contacts to your other contacts in the same industry.

Did You Know?
Israel exports 65% of its (cut) diamonds to the U.S.

Finally, it's often worthwhile to suggest having an Israeli organization cosign or cosponsor any proclamation your organization is releasing to the press – particularly when it comes to neutral, non-political, ones. Getting the public used to seeing Israeli organizations on such proclamations helps, however minutely, in having people view Israel as just one more normal country.

THINGS YOU CAN DO TODAY:

1. Join any organization that interests you – and try to join key committees and the staff of any publications or newsletters that organization releases.
2. Introduce your Israeli contacts to your non-Israeli contacts, especially at conferences.
3. Reach out to Israeli non profits and exchange website links. Put out a joint press release announcing formal cooperation between your organizations.
4. Suggest a free Israeli channel day to your cable or satellite provider. If they don't offer an Israeli channel – suggest one.
5. Ask Israeli organizations to cosponsor and co-draft proclamations and declarations, or at least to sign off on them.
6. Sponsor a local Israeli **Independence Day** event. It can be as elaborate as a parade or as simple as a display of Israeli art or music in the park. Ask an Israeli mayor for help.
7. Think about hosting a summer camp for Israeli kids. Or sending local kids to a camp in Israel. Create a program.
8. Get involved in student exchange programs with Israel. If one doesn't exist already – suggest creating one to your local colleges and universities.
9. Consider setting up a faculty exchange with Israeli schools or universities.
10. Ask your elected representatives to consider joining with Israeli Members of Knesset on joint projects.
11. Suggest that your city twin an Israeli city, town or kibbutz. Go to **www.sister-cities.org** for a partial list of such twins.
12. Ask the government for funds to help business and cultural connections between your city and the Israeli twin.

PART 4

CAMPUS ACTIVISM

9. Helping Israel on Campus: The College Years

It was my first year in university and I went to hear someone from a famous organization speak about a topic that I thought was incredibly important (I won't go into the details, to avoid embarrassing the organization). The speaker was excellent, riled us up about all the terrible things that we should be outraged about – and then left us with nothing to do about it.

Never willing to be passive, I made an appointment with the speaker to meet him at his office the next day and offer to volunteer. To my shock, he not only reiterated that there was no constructive activity that I could do as a student, but proceeded to tell me that he had no need for any volunteers.

This chapter is meant to be an antidote to that kind of thinking.

For most of us the college years play a crucial part in shaping our world views for decades to come. It is also, generally, the last time we have the time, energy and passion to devote to ideas and causes purely on their merits. So it is ever so important that we encourage college students to tap into their energy to help Israel now, on campus.

Considering the stakes, it's no surprise that college campuses today are virtual battlefields, with pro-Israel and anti-Israel forces clashing their verbal sabers against one another at every opportunity. But besides addressing outright propaganda (and see the chapter **Becoming a Spokesperson for Israel** and the chapter **Fighting anti-Israel Forms of anti-Semitism**), there are a myriad of ways to be active in helping Israel on campus. And that's true whether you're a student or an older member of the community.

I. FOR STUDENTS

Influencing the Content of Courses

Just because you're a student doesn't mean that you're powerless. You not only vote with your feet every time you choose to take (or not take) a course, but you can provide on-the-spot feedback about those courses.

When professors in courses have opinions, take notice of what they're saying. If there are some who are advocating Israel's destruction or who have turned their classes into a fest of Israel-bashing, speak up! Talk to the administration, to parents and donors – and to other students. Start an on-campus or internet campaign of protest, if what the professor is advocating has crossed the line into outright anti-Semitism. There's just no reason to spend a fortune on courses that force you to endure bile.

Sponsor Events on Campus

In addition to trying to influence course content, students can also influence what ideas are being discussed on campus by organizing events that take place on college grounds.

Start by inviting Israeli or Israel-oriented speakers to student unions, clubs, fraternities and events. Include non-political speakers whenever possible – authors, artists, musicians, chemists, business people, computer programmers – many of these can draw an audience and be helpful.

Screen Israeli films, hold debates about Israeli policy (policy – not legitimacy), bring in pro-Israel politicians to address groups of "future leaders" (start with politicians who are alumni, if there are any), organize any kind of fair and include products from Israel – and don't forget to publicize the event in flyers that are Israel-friendly.

Five Ways to Help Israel that Also Just Might Impress a Date:

1. Take them to see a cool Israeli band or singer.
2. Cook them the best dinner ever, with Israeli recipes and foods (alternatively, take them to a fancy Israeli restaurant, if one is nearby).
3. Pour them a drink of an award-winning Israeli wine.
4. Take them to a black tie event where you're the speaker, talking about Middle East politics.
5. Make a fortune in Israeli hi-tech stocks.

Make New Friends

Hands down the best way for students to influence other students is through social contact – so make yourself uncomfortable if necessary and make new friends. Get on the boards of student committees, join the staff of the school's newspaper or radio, join any and all kinds of groups or even unions, get online and join facebook or any newer internet sites – and start talking to people. It's ever so much easier to suggest a book or a movie to a friend than to some nameless co-ed walking by in a rush.

Set a goal: Make one new friend a month.

Make Friends with a Professor

It's tough to be friends with a professor – but definitely worthwhile, both for your career and your ability to influence things on campus. And if "friends" seems like too much, just ask some questions once a month after class and get to know them as a person.

Get Involved in Local Politics

It's never too early or too late to get involved in local politics, from the smallest neighborhood councils to the largest munici- pality. Local politics is often overlooked but local politicians can have a great deal of say within a city – and on the local college campuses. Even for those of us who have no interest in joining, fundraising or volunteering for any of the major parties running our town, it would behoove all of us to get to know the people behind the scenes. These are, after all, people who both have some power today and may amass a great deal later if their careers are successful.

Politicians are almost always keen to accept any kind of free help (especially from students they can try to "mold") so my advice here is to find some cause – Israel related or not – and volunteer to help out with this cause from the office(s) of those in charge. Best bet: find out which causes are already dear to their hearts (start by searching online) and then offer a few hours a week. If you so much as just show up regularly, within a year you might just be their best friend.

Don't Forget Student Politics

Whether it's a student union or the college branch of your favorite national party, here's a chance to get to know and influence both the school and the nation's next generation of leaders.

Fundraise for an Apolitical Israeli Charity

We are creatures who want to be consistent and we are great rationalizers, which is why once we've donated something – anything, frankly, from an hour of our time to a button from our coats – we follow up by finding reasons to support the person or cause we've donated to. In other words, psychology rules.

So, applying this principle, we can see that perhaps the most effective way to get someone to start seeing Israel as having basic legitimacy is to persuade that person to donate even one measly dollar to any Israeli charity. The very act of giving has an impact far greater than the cash.

Since we're after long-term warm feelings for the Jewish State irrespective of politics, I'd suggest trying to get money for apolitical charities. Think hospitals, schools and services for the Israeli disabled (and see the resources list at the back of the book for ideas). To start, contact one of these organizations and get some literature. After that, just set up a table anywhere where students walk by and try to get as many popular or good-looking students to stand around and man the tables. If you want to really get into the spirit of luring in the unwary, offer free food to go along with any amount of donation – no minimum required. Who can say no to a slice of pizza with a cute girl/guy and the chance to feel that you've given something to the needy?

Did You Know?
Albert Einstein was offered, and turned down, the Israeli presidency in 1952. In his Will, however, Einstein bequeathed the rights to his writings to The Hebrew University of Jerusalem.

Hold Parties or Food Fairs with Israeli Music

You can go all out and import an Israeli band, or get the local music major to bring a guitar – or even, in a pinch, rely on recorded music – but anything with an Israeli theme should get people asking what kind of music you're all listening to.

While you're planning the party, by the way, don't forget to buy Israeli food – maybe even make it into a full-fledged food fair, featuring different cultures as well (and giving you a chance to join up with other students of different cultures and ethnicities to plan it). And you might want to consider buying tiny Israeli flags on toothpicks to spear the food.

And if you're feeling particularly patriotic to Israel you can send some Israeli soldiers a pizza from the party. No joke – there's a website (**pizzaIDF.org**) that will do this.

Take Advantage of the University Blogosphere

Students are usually the first to know which blogs and websites are the most trafficked and popular. Get to know them – and contribute your two cents worth on any topic. By the time an Israel-related topic comes up, your name will already have credibility.

Give Israeli Gifts

Whether for Christmas or Hanukkah, for your sweetheart or for that professor you're trying to bribe, consider buying a gift made in Israel. Dead Sea cosmetics, chocolate, jewelry, or wine are all viable options.

Go to or Organize Retreats

A good way to meet new people, learn something and support Israel all at the same time is to go to or organize a weekend retreat that has an Israel-related theme. Or even just a brief lecture. Democracy in the Middle East, the effect of the Dead Sea Scrolls on Christianity, how to flirt with Israelis – all great topics to think about bringing up on your weekend away.

Get and Give Feedback to the Local Community

Sometimes the college students and the local community around the school are worried about the same things – but don't talk to each other. Don't let that be you! Go to local community events that aren't college oriented. Who knows? You may even find that you like some of the locals. Better yet, set up a once a month meeting with some of the local leaders, perhaps at a restaurant or coffee shop.

Display pro-Israel Messages

Wear an Israeli t-shirt, put up flyers that are pro-Israel, have a "buy Israeli" campaign, have fact-sheets available on a table, carry around a pro-Israel book, put up photographs of beautiful Israeli landscapes – anything that gets Israel out to the audience in a positive (preferably non-invasive) way. Make yourself a source of information for other students who may be interested but who won't go looking for answers on their own.

And if you don't have the answers yourself (especially to counter an anti-Israel campaign) then ask organizations and search online and get their fact-sheets and flyers.

One caveat: remember that perception stays with us a lot longer than information. It's more important to be seen as calm, rational, intelligent, and normal – than to shout out the best answer you've ever heard in a voice ten decibels higher than a banshee. This is especially important to keep in mind at rallies, sit-ins and other events that sometimes get out of hand.

Sell pro-Israel Books

Here's a thought for making a bit of money and doing some good at the same time – find used books about Israel (people moving homes and jettisoning excess materials are a great source) and sell them cheap. Ditto for Israeli movies, photos, etc.

A Few Resources:

- *Myths and Facts about Israel*, online: *www.jewishvirtuallibrary.org/jsource/myths/mftoc.html*
- *www.camera.org (tracking accuracy in the media)*
- *www.worldjewishcongress.org*
- *www.wujs.org.il (Worldwide Jewish students union)*
- *www.campus-watch.org*
- *Israel on campus coalition (http://israelcc.org).*
- *Hillel (www.hillel.org).*
- *Dershowitz, Alan. The Case for Israel (Wiley, 2004).*
- *Hertzberg, Arthur. The Zionist Idea: A Historical Analysis and Reader (Jewish Publication Society, 1997).*

> • Oren, Michael B. *Six Days of War: June 1967
> and the Making of the Modern Middle East*
> *(Presidio, 2003).*
> *For more resources check the resources list in the back
> of the book.*

Learn One New Fact Each Week

Decide to research one new fact about Israel each week. After
all, you can never know too much. And here's a thought: do the
research in the school's library; you never know who you might
end up talking to – and wouldn't that be a funny "hey, you know
how we met?" story?

Organize an "Israel Week"

If you have the energy, here's an idea I think is a real winner: an
"Israel Week," where you run seminars, parties, discussions and
movies about Israel for one day at each university or campus in
your area for a week. Concentrating on one campus per day lets
you focus your energy on each location as well as being able to
take the same people and props to different campuses the following days.

Start an Israel Club

Start or join an Israel club. Invite anyone with an interest and
brainstorm once a week about ways to promote the country.
Also a good way to meet new and interesting people.

Have a Blue-and-White Day

Have a blue-and-white day, where everyone wears Israel's national colors. Then speak to anyone who asks about it. To make this
truly effective, you need numbers: so advertise it widely in
advance. If you want to be less subtle, pin a small Israeli flag on
your lapel.

Organize a Debate

Organize a debate about Israeli policies. Yes, this would be polit-ical – so choose your sides in whatever moves you. Don't be shy about controversy here – a debate gives you a chance to talk to people you otherwise wouldn't. The only rule here is to be sure that the debate is not over Israel's basic right to exist – that should be taken for granted, and hopefully will be if you focus on policy alone.

Visit Israel

It will never be cheaper for you to travel than when you're a stu-dent. In some cases, it may even be free (see, for example, the resources list at the back of the book for fellowships and pro-grams such as **Birthright**). But whatever the expense, it's well worth it if you can swing a trip to Israel even once during your college years. You'll learn a lot, see the county from a perspec-tive never talked about on the news and maybe meet a few Israelis to argue with (er, get friendly with).

The Birthright Israel program
is one of the best ideas our time has seen.
Sheldon Adelson,
Adelson Family Charitable Foundation

Just whatever you do, don't forget to bring back souvenirs! The merchants will love you, the knick-knacks will make great conversation starters and, besides, all your long-lost "friends" will want gifts anyway.

II. FOR PARENTS AND OTHER NON-STUDENTS

Influencing the Content of Courses

As a parent or other non-student, the most effective way of helping Israel on campus is to try to influence the infrastructure, if you will, of the college experience.

Ultimately, what students learn in college is heavily influenced by what courses they take, what books they're required to read, what essays they have to write – and what their professors will reward them for saying (or, conversely, penalize them for advocating).

Regardless of where our politics lie with respect to the policies of this or that Israeli administration, our goal should be that it is a given, in college courses and on campus, that Israel has a right to exist as a Jewish State and chart the course of its own future. This starts with the content of the courses and the choice of professors to teach them.

Although most students don't have much direct say over courses, parents and donors to the university do. As do politicians, retired faculty, and others who influence the curriculum or set it. The first thing to do, then, is get to know the decision-makers for our local colleges and for the schools that we or our children attend and understand who they are and how best to influence them.

Once the decision-makers are identified, we can start to suggest courses that are interesting, academically rigorous and intellectual, and that include the basic assumption of Israel's right to exist or at least the reading of books that reinforce that idea. Thus, a course that discusses the proper diplomatic course that Israel should take with regard to Lebanon (for instance) would start with the premise that Israel has the right to have a diplomatic agenda, as would any other normal country. Regardless of what politics might ensue, at least the basic right to exist would be reinforced. Similarly, a workshop that explores the hypothetical effect on the European economy of an oil pipeline from Iraq through Jordan and then Israel (terminating at Haifa's port) carries with it the unspoken conviction that Israel should have a port in Haifa.

If a brand new course is difficult to pitch, suggest books and audiovisual materials to professors who are teaching existing courses. The obvious place to start is within the departments teaching politics or Middle East studies (and for ideas about which books or materials, see the resources list at the back of this book or contact some pro-Israel organizations), but there are ways of beefing up non-political courses with Israeli content too. A course discussing any aspect of law might benefit from inclusion of a comparison with Israeli law. Art courses can include a module focusing on Israeli artists. Science courses can have Israeli research publications included in their list of mandatory readings. Psychology courses might want to include a section about Israeli victims of terror and post traumatic stress syndrome.

Similarly, in any given field there are Israeli academics that have expertise. Suggest that the university invite some of them to be visiting professors or just to give a one-time lecture, class or seminar. If the budget is unavailable, perhaps the community can pitch in and cover part of the costs. When Israelis are visiting for any reason, it's worth finding out whether a talk to university students is feasible. First choice would be in a class or being sponsored by the college, but talking to a student union, club or even at a nearby pub or café would work too.

Of course, discuss all this with students. Although it's more difficult for a student to exert pressure, it is, after all, their education we're talking about.

Make Friends with the Donors

Other than trying to influence course content, talking to major donors gives you the opportunity to suggest ways for them to feel involved in Israel without too much difficulty. One way:

suggest that they consider donating money to the school in the form of **State of Israel Bonds**. Other possibilities: suggesting that the school invite them to speak on campus about their area of expertise – and thus giving them a chance to discuss Israel, too, if it's appropriate.

Talk to the School about Israeli Partners

If you don't know or want to get to know the present donors, maybe speak to the school and suggest Israeli companies that the school might be interested in either partnering with or asking for a donation or ad from (or possibly investing in). The more Israeli companies donate to the university, the more likely the university will be to listen to Israelis.

Beef Up a Student's Resumé

Whether it's for your own child or someone else's, you can help them beef up their resumé and help Israel simultaneously by putting them in touch with pro-Israel charities, non-profits and companies and suggesting that they work there part-time during college (whether for pay or as an intern). Who says you can't help Israel and yourself at the same time?

Send Your Kids to the Right Schools

Of course the most obvious and powerful weapon that parents have in influencing their children's education is simply choosing to send them to (or persuading them to choose) schools that provide both a good education and a pro-Israel atmosphere already.

THINGS YOU CAN DO TODAY:

1. Listen to the professors and their opinions – and notice who says what. Make sure that if someone says something that impugns Israel's very right to exist, the students, administration, university donors and local community know about it. But don't call a press conference – it just makes the

powers-that-be defensive and then the chances of getting rid of that professor drop like a lead weight.

2. Decide to make one new friend every month. Expand your friendships – and you'll expand your influence. Talk to the person sitting next to you in class.

3. Suggest a pro-Israel book to one of your new friends or colleagues.

4. Carry around a pro-Israel book in your hand. This can be a great conversation-starter with new people you meet.

5. Wear a pro-Israel t-shirt, button, hat. Put one on your car or bike. Download flyers from the Internet or make them up yourself.

6. Make up buttons, flyers, posters that say "Buy Israeli" – and suggest good Israeli products to people who ask.

7. Get online. Start a blog. Join online communities. Find people who share your hobbies and interests and talk about Israel – later.

8. Decide to research one new fact about Israel each week. Do the research in the school's library.

9. Screen an Israeli film for students.

10. Have fact-sheets available to students who want to know about Israel. Make them easy to find. Put up a table, put them down at entrances to buildings or distribute them by hand.

11. Sell Israeli music, movies, books, art. Ask locals to donate used ones and sell 'em cheap.

12. Have a blue-and-white day, where everyone wears Israel's national colors. Then speak to anyone who asks about it.

13. Approach student clubs of different ethnicities, nationalities or religions – and invite them to do a joint event. This can be as simple as having a film night with a double feature (one Israeli) or as elaborate as hosting multiple performers on stage from different countries or races.

14. Invite Israeli students to your events and parties. If you don't know any, ask around at the Jewish unions and clubs.

15. Join student unions.

16. Join the student wings of national political parties. Or at least make friends with some of the people who do.

17. Bring in Israeli music and bands. Have a party, hold a sing-a-thon, do an Israeli song version of American Idol. Be creative.

18. Buy Israeli food and talk about it with people. Put little Israeli flags (on toothpicks) in falafels and set up a cheap falafel stand. For that matter, put those flag-toothpicks on other stuff too!

19. Start to fundraise for a non-political Israeli charity (think hospitals, homes for the aged). The goal should be to get people to donate anything – regardless of how small. One possibility: set up a table, with free candy, cookies or other food, and make it look like a fun place to hang out.

20. Organize a fair – it can be an arts fair, music fair, food fair or anything else. Then make sure that Israeli products are represented. Perhaps have an Israeli booth at the fair.

21. Get on the board of any student committee. If you're a parent, get on the board of any committee for parents.

22. Join the staff of the school's newspaper and/or radio or other media. Contribute an article about Israel to the paper.

23. Organize a debate about Israeli policies. Don't be shy about controversy – it gives you a chance to talk to people you otherwise wouldn't.

24. Organize an "Israel Week," where you run seminars, parties, discussions and movies about Israel for one day at each university or campus in your area for a week.

25. Bring in pro-Israel politicians to speak on campus. Start with nationally known names, especially if any of them are alumni. Then go for local politicos.

26. Find out who the local politicians are – municipal and neighborhood. Then offer to volunteer a few hours a week.

27. Have a regular dialogue between students and the local community. Set up a once a month meeting in a restaurant. Make it part of everyone's routine. Start the first one off next week.

28. Find a way to plan a trip to Israel. Youth prices, trips funded by fellowships, studying abroad – it'll never be easier than when you're a student.

29. Start or join an Israel club. Invite anyone with an interest and brainstorm once a week about ways to promote the country.

30. Suggest to donors that they donate their money in the form of **Israel Bonds**.
31. Suggest Israeli companies that the school might be interested in either funding, partnering with or asking for a donation or ad from.
32. Decide to make friends with one professor – in any subject.
33. Find out who the donors are to the university and where they hang out. Start going to those places too. Make friends with one donor.
34. Pitch ideas to the university for courses that focus on Israel or Israel's influence on the Middle East.
35. Suggest books and audiovisual materials to professors who already teach courses where Israel is a focus.
36. Suggest Israeli materials (books, research studies, art, etc) to professors teaching general courses. This is especially easy to do for the sciences, as Israel has many top of the line professors writing in academic journals.
37. Suggest names of Israeli experts to be visiting professors, teach part of a course, or to give one-time lectures or seminars. Experts can be in any field – from art to politics to physics. Talk to the Israeli Consulate for names.
38. If the administration isn't interested in inviting Israeli experts – invite them yourself. Set it up in a local café, art museum, hotel conference room, or even someone's house. Charge a nominal admission price, if necessary, to help with costs.

PART 5

MONEY MATTERS

10. Donating Money and Fundraising Ideas

I've always been a bit uncomfortable about all the fundraising for Israel. The image of the Jewish State, with its hand outstretched, pleading for cash, is at such odds with the vision of a strong and independent country, with a bright future, that it's jarring. It's also upsetting for anyone who believes that Jews from around the world should consider moving there, since it's frankly hard to psych people up to potentially move to a country that's consistently portrayed as a charity case.

On the other hand, there's no denying that the money donated to Israel over the years has helped the Jewish State to survive. In the early years the money was crucial. And even today, when the amount of money donated is small compared to Israel's GDP, there's no shortage of good uses (even critically important uses) for donated monies. Simply put, donating money is still one of the easiest and most directly effective ways to help Israel continue to survive, even today.

I. DONATING YOUR OWN MONEY

Choosing from Different Kinds of Charity

There are lots of charities out there that help Israel and if you're looking to donate money, you can find a myriad of them online or in any local Jewish community's newspaper ads. Broadly speaking, though, there are different kinds of charity. There are those organizations that help Israel by supporting its infrastructure – planting trees, investing in public projects such as water purification, and building shelters, those that help indigent Israelis – bringing food to their tables or clothes and other necessities, those that are focused on local Israeli versions of global causes, such as the environment or climate control, those that focus on education, those that specialize in dealing with the medical needs of Israelis, and, of course, all those nonprofits that focus on politics but still manage to retain their charitable organization status.

If you're looking for a place to start giving, then, I'd suggest deciding on the category of charity that you support the most, and then finding one of the Israeli versions of that category. Ideally, of course, you might want to aspire to finding a charity in each category that you can consider supporting.

Just to get you started, a few of the most well-known charities supporting Israel are the **Jewish Agency**, **UJA-Federation** (now called **UJC**), **Magen David Adom** (the Israeli version of the **Red Cross**), the **Joint Distribution Committee (JDC)**, **AIPAC**, **Hadassah**, and **Yad Sarah** (medical equipment distribution). For some more prominent names, and a few not-so-prominent ones, check out the by-no-means-comprehensive list in the resources section in the back of this book.

Did You Know?

The city of Netanya, in Northern Israel, was named after philanthropist Nathan Straus, who was the 19th century co-owner of Macy's in New York.

Group Charity

Sometimes it's easier and better to donate as a group, rather than alone. You might want to approach your company, church, synagogue, or book reading club to donate something together, as a unit. This takes the pressure off any one person and also allows the group to sponsor a bigger project. A small example of this approach would be asking your company to undertake sponsoring one Israeli family in need for a year. (One charity already doing this is the **Israel Emergency Solidarity Fund – One Family** with their **"Embrace"** program for families who are victims of terror.) The group approach also allows for closer emotional attachment and feelings of responsibility towards the charitable project without breaking anyone's bank account.

Giving Automatically

Setting up systems whereby some of your money goes to an Israeli charity without you having to think about it each time is a great way of increasing your charity with relatively little time consumption. For example, set up your checking account to donate a small amount each month to the charity of your choice, or for your employer to cut a check once a year (perhaps a portion of any bonus would be a good place to start this, as by definition you can probably do without at least some of a bonus).

Shopping at a store or company which promises to give a percentage to charity is another example. If you're a business, sending out coupons to the public where they are promised a charity discount (10% going to charity, for example) allows you to donate money and drive traffic to your business simultaneously.

Finally, I've long thought that it would be a good idea for some of the charities out there to team up with the companies offering credit cards – and perhaps create a "blue and white" credit card, where some of the fees and income generated by using the card would be sent to Israel. And it turns out that while I was merely thinking at least one company went and implemented this idea: Check out **www.hasadvantage.com** for details.

Donations in Kind

It doesn't always have to be cold cash. Often, we have plenty of stuff in our homes that we no longer need – and simply end up throwing out. Whether we're moving homes, doing a spring cleaning or just upgrading to the latest version, we're constantly junking items that are perfectly usable for other, less fortunate, souls.

Sometimes there are charities that are designed to collect (and maybe even pick up) these items and we can donate them directly (used clothes is a good example). But often there seems to be no easy way to do this. So I suggest the following: if your city doesn't have an organization doing this already, set up a "flea market" once or twice a year. During the course of the year everyone with expendable stuff drops off their wares at an office or warehouse and then the whole community volunteers to man booths at the flea market which then sells these to the public. With the proceeds, of course, going to Israel. This is a great way to give charity, get the whole community involved in a group project, get rid of stuff you don't need, and have fun. If you really do this right, you can arrange for the local press to give free advertising both to the flea market itself and to the charity.

If all this seems like too much work, well, you can always just have a garage sale.

Send a Gift of a Donation

Having trouble figuring out what to give people as a gift? Why not give a donation on their behalf? (One good example: donating the planting of a tree in Israel; check out the **Jewish National Fund** for details.) You feel good, they feel good and Israel benefits. And, as an added bonus, you can give the same gift to many people.

Donating After Death

Written your will yet? Why not leave something to a charity that will help Israel? Better yet, why not donate it now as a lifetime trust? Talk to your tax advisor(s), or ask to talk to your favorite charity's planned giving specialists, and figure out the best way to enjoy your property/income when you're alive, have a great tax write-off, and give a lot of gelt to the Jewish State all at the same time.

II. DONATING OTHER PEOPLE'S MONEY (FUNDRAISING)

So you don't have any money. You're a student, unemployed, a struggling artist, have high expenses, little income, or no savings. But there are charities out there calling to you. So what's a body to do? Fundraise, of course.

Now, some people are naturals when it comes to fundraising. Energy and ideas just ooze from their pores effortlessly. Cold calls are fun. Other people will shrink to pea-size just by contemplating the idea. Cold calls can make them sweat until they need cold showers. If you fall into the latter category, don't be worried – cold calls are not the only way to raise money for a good cause.

One hint, by the way, when it comes to fundraising: always have a defined goal. If you have a number in mind that you're aiming for, you're much more likely to get it.

Getting Other People Involved

Those who work in the fundraising business know that it's not only about the dollars (or Euros, Pounds, etc.). The challenge today seems to be less the raising of actual cash (there are a few very rich people giving donations) than the challenge of increasing the number of people giving even small amounts.

> *Our lives begin to end the day*
> *we become silent about things that matter.*
> **Martin Luther King Jr.**

As any politician will tell you, someone who gives even one dollar to a campaign is more likely to feel committed to it. As such, it behooves us to figure out ways of getting people who are currently not involved to give at least a tiny amount to an Israeli charity of their choice.

Possible ways of doing this (besides the nagging telemarketers and junk mail) can include putting small charity boxes in public places, running targeted campaigns asking for small amounts of money, and asking businesses to donate some leftover change at the end of each day. Proliferating the number of projects that a charitable organization conducts can also work since the more projects out there the more people there are who may connect emotionally to at least one of them.

Which brings us to the point of transparency. The more transparent a charity is about where the money is going, the easier it will be to raise it – and to keep people feeling involved as well as attracting more people to donate.

Incidentally, this might be a good time to suggest that if you or someone you know works for any charity organization (including those not remotely related to Israel) there may be an opportunity for some cross-cultural connecting. That is, it's probably easier to convince a donor who's already giving money to a European charity dedicated to saving the planet to up the ante and give a few Euro to an Israeli charity doing the same.

Throw a Party

Hands down the most fun way to raise money is to just charge admission for a party that everyone wants to go to anyway. Then advertise – heavily – that part or all of the admission price is going to charity. With any luck, you'll draw an even bigger crowd than usual. To do this with relative ease, you might want to consider teaming up with one or more organizations ahead of time, to get the benefit of their name recognition – and their mailing lists. Don't forget wine-tasting parties and sports parties in this category.

Have an Auction

Chinese or regular, auctions raise money and people enjoy going to them. To maximize the event, approach local businesses for items to donate ahead of time.

Get Your Children Involved

Exploit your kids! Get them to join the fundraising effort by selling candy, hitting up their teachers, or putting on a doleful face for strangers. Better yet, get the whole school involved (giving the school a slice of the net, probably) by suggesting a carnival, competitions between classes (who can sell the most sodas, for instance, or design the most creative websites for kids), or a talent show with a charge for admission.

Hit Up Your Company

It's tax deductible, it smacks of good PR, and it's a way to feel good – ask your boss to get the company to pony up a small donation. Be sure to ask for a charity that's apolitical, such as an Israeli environmental organization or educational institute (see the resources list at the back of the book). If he's a real sport, organize a company "carnival" where for a dollar or two workers can try to hit the boss with a pie in the kisser. That ought to bring in some dough!

Sell Food

Whether it's hotdogs at a sports game or baked cakes at your church, selling food is a great fundraiser. And don't forget the chocolate. Always chocolate.

Charge for Something Silly

Have a casual day at work – for people who fork over five dollars (which you donate, obviously). Put up a kissing booth on campus. Collect a buck for the right to express an opinion at your book club. Sell funny hats. Have an "ugly" pageant or "funny costume" pageant and charge for admission. Fill an enormous glass jar with coins. Wallpaper a wall of your office with dollar bills – when you finish the wall send it to charity. You get the idea.

Create and Sell Paraphernalia

Whether it's a calendar (pictures of Israel, anyone?), a mug, buttons, t-shirts, or customized bracelets, if you can create an Israeli theme and then sell it – you'll raise money. Want to go all out? Ask everyone you know to donate something specific (for example, a chair or a windbreaker) decorated as creatively as possible, and then hold a sale of all of these on one night. With any luck, people's creative and competitive streaks will arise and buyers will have many interesting (and useful) chairs or jackets to choose from.

Do a Car Wash

This is old faithful. The easiest way to raise funds quickly and have fun, if it's good weather and you do it with friends.

Hold a Walk-a-thon (or any other "thon")

Gather pledges and corporate sponsors and have a "thon." Whether it's walking, running, climbing or learning, these are time-tested ways of collecting money for a cause.

Recycle for Cash

Gather your friends and start collecting anything recyclable that can be returned for cash. Be it bottles or print cartridges, there's money to be raised from stuff we usually just discard.

Online Fundraising

Got a website? Make it easy for people to give a little charity at the click of a mouse, by adding a donate-per-click button, or a link to a charity that has one.

Discount Cards and Scratch Cards

Contact a supplier of these cards, which are basically books of coupons from national merchants, and then sell 'em! Discount cards are usually sold for a flat fee (for example $10 for a book of cards that have coupons worth much more than that) and scratch cards have an element of fun – you scratch the card first to reveal the amount that you agree to donate.

The trick to selling these is to remember to tell the people you're soliciting where the money is going and why that particular charity needs it.

Selling Honor(s)

This is especially good for churches and synagogues – create visual recognitions (plaques, for instance) for major donors and minor ones (name announcements) for smaller donors. Hook up with a charity and have the charity recognize the donors on their website too.

Gamble

Well, don't gamble – charge for gambling. That is, run a poker game or a mini-casino. As long as you don't do it illegally, there's lots of moola to make for a good cause.

THINGS YOU CAN DO TODAY:

1. Put a small charity box for an Israeli charity in a public place – like your office or the corner coffee shop. This is an easier sell if the shop is located near a synagogue or Christian Zionist church.
2. Put a small amount aside each week to donate to Israel.
3. Plant a tree in Israel. Check out the **Jewish National Fund** or go to **http://192.116.234.203/kkl/index.asp** for details.
4. Make a donation in someone else's name, as a gift.
5. Don't forget to donate used clothes, cars, and other in-kind donations.
6. Donate your professional services to a charity working for Israel.
7. Add a "donate by clicking here" button on your website(s).
8. Don't forget to include Israeli charities in your will.
9. Contribute as part of a group – through your synagogue, church, business, or community center.

10. Ask a business if they'd be willing to donate leftover change to charity. Then contact a charity and tell them.
11. Advertise that you'll donate a portion of your business revenue to charity (and then do it, of course).
12. Throw a fundraising party. The key is to make them fun, so that people won't mind paying the admission charge.
13. Hold a fundraising brainstorming session with your friends and neighbors.
14. Have an auction, with the proceeds going to Israel.
15. Have a contest, with or without kids involved, and donate the profits.
16. Ask your boss to give to an apolitical Israeli charity, on the company's behalf.
17. Have a bake sale. Or sell hot dogs, cookies, candies, etc.
18. Put up a kissing booth.
19. Charge for the right to dress casually at work, once a month.
20. Sell mugs, calendars, bumper stickers and the like.
21. Do a car wash. Don't forget to advertise.
22. Hold a walk-a-thon (or learn-a-thon, or any other "thon").
23. Sell discount cards and scratch cards.
24. Sell honors at your place of worship or at work.
25. Run a poker game, lotto or casino, so long as it's legal.
26. Consider donating money via a trust (talk to financial professionals).
27. Set up a flea market, with the proceeds to go to Israel. This can be a community fundraiser, once a year or more.

PART 6

SPIRITUAL
CONNECTIONS

11. Strengthening National and Spiritual Ties – Jews

Israelis traveling the world who want to feel a taste of home know better than to try to find it in any Israeli embassy or consulate, full of serious diplomats. Instead, they drop themselves off at the nearest Jewish community center or synagogue, where they're almost certain to find the same kind of tastes, sounds and chutzpa of the Jewish State, miniaturized and compressed into a single building: the rabbi, head of a synagogue where everyone considers themselves more qualified; the person in charge of public relations, who detests speaking to people; the community caterer, who insists on telling you what foods you really like. It's no exaggeration to say that Israelis and Jews worldwide treat one another like extended family – even, sometimes, to the point of dysfunction.

In a word, then, the most natural, organic, supporters of the Jewish State are the Jews scattered around the world. So it only stands to reason that anything that buffers up Jews' connections to being part of the Jewish people also helps Israel.

In addition, there's every reason to try to capitalize on the already strong connection that spiritually connected Jews feel towards Judaism and ensure that there's a strong spiritual connection to the people of Israel as well.

I. CONNECTING JEWS
TO OTHER JEWS & TO JUDAISM

Invite Your Unaffiliated Friends

Probably the easiest way to strengthen the Jewish people is to simply invite a fellow Jew to come with you to a synagogue or to a Jewish event. Whether it's a lecture, a play, a musical, a singles party, a movie, a religious holiday, a Shabbat meal, or a community fundraiser, simply mingling socially with other Jews and having the opportunity to ask a knowledgeable member of the tribe some questions, has the potential to do wonders. And hopefully you'll enjoy the food, too!

Subscribe to a Community or Israeli Magazine or Newsletter

Whether you read them online or have them delivered by your local snail postal service, nothing beats a newspaper or magazine for staying in the gossip loop of a community. And what better way is there to feel a part of your community than to know its skeletons?

Seriously, though, staying current with the local Jewish news and the Israeli news will not only give you conversation fodder for the water cooler, it will keep you informed of local events, business opportunities and educational possibilities. Definitely worth signing up.

Join a Community Center

Jewish community centers can definitely be a bit pricey, but they offer so many programs and chances to strengthen the community that they're well worth it. From sports programs to after-school curricula and cultural events many of these centers are stupendous. Grab a friend and get thee to a community center!

Look Out for Business Networking Opportunities

There are Jews out there aggressively networking with other Jews for professional and business reasons – why not be one of them? One example is the J2J networking service on the internet (see **j2jnetworking.org**). Helping a fellow Jew succeed binds each of you closer to each other and to the community too. Besides, if you have more money, you'll be more inclined to give more charity.

Support an Outreach Organization

If your time and/or wallet can afford it, there are plenty of organizations out there willing to have you help them reach out to Jews who have little to no Jewish background. Many of these organizations have amazing resources and events, from in-depth websites which answer questions to organized trips to Israel.

In the Orthodox world examples include **Chabad**, **Aish HaTorah**, **Gateways**, and **Ohr Somayach**; for Conservative Jews, the **United Synagogue** for Conservative Judaism offers **KOACH** for college students; and in the Reform movement the **Union for Reform Judaism** offers an official **Outreach Program**. For more info see the resources list at the back of the book.

Organize a Social Event

Organizing a social event geared for Jews can be a great opportunity to expand your circle of friends and help the Jewish people all at once. This is especially true if you're single. One word of advice: make the event an enjoyable one even if you don't meet Mr. or Ms. Right.

Commit to Expanding Your Education

There's a plethora of opportunities to become one of those knowledgeable members of the tribe, if you're not one already (and an even more knowledgeable one if you are). Look out for summer camps, weekend retreats, lectures, courses and even libraries full of academic journals — and then just make yourself available to answer your friends' questions. You'll help the unaffiliated and meet new community members simultaneously.

Volunteer Within the Community

Hands down the quickest way to get to know your local community — and be welcomed into it if you're new — is to volunteer any amount of time whatsoever.

Volunteer possibilities are virtually endless, considering the number of schools, medical centers, charity organizations, old age homes, vocational services, and children's services that each sizable community runs. And most of them can be found just by searching the phone book or internet in your area. A quick phone call (ask for whoever is in charge of volunteers) and you could be making a difference within days. The key, of course, to good volunteering is to offer to do something that you think is either important or something you enjoy (or both). Don't be afraid of grunt work but do offer to contribute work that you think will help them and won't look half bad on a résumé.

Incidentally, I do believe that it would behoove the Jewish community as a whole to get into the habit of sending our graduates into some kind of community service work for a semester or two. Israelis commit to years of army service — shouldn't Diaspora 18 year olds be encouraged to give a semester? Or perhaps 10 hours per week for a year? Maybe if we gave them a certificate at the end of it, with awards for the top volunteers. Or the possibility of a scholarship. Just a thought.

II. CONNECTING SPIRITUALLY TO ISRAEL

Prayers in Synagogues

According to the Talmud, all Jews are connected to each other. And that certainly includes those who live in Israel. So why not add in a few prayers for those brethren who dwell there? It certainly can't hurt. Whether it's a chapter of Psalms, or a *misheberach* for Israeli soldiers, connecting religiously to Israelis can only help increase the odds of Israeli survival.

And while you're at the synagogue don't forget that tradition has it that any Jewish learning you do helps too.

Did You Know?
The largest stone in the Western Wall in Jerusalem has a length of more than 40 feet, a width of over 10 feet and is estimated to weigh 570 tons. This is heavier than any stone in the Egyptian pyramids!

Check in by Remote

These days you don't have to fly to Israel to see the Western Wall. You can even write a note to be placed in its cracks – and do it all online. Check out **www.thekotel.org** or **aish.com/wallcam** – they're great Kotel cams.

Play Jewish Trivial Pursuit

Another in-home idea: have a "Jewish Trivia" night. Find a commercial Jewish Trivial Pursuit game, or simply search the internet for trivia and make up your own game of trivial pursuit for your friends. And then, if you're feeling spunky, post the humorous answers on youtube...

Bake a Jewish Dish

Feeling hungry for material nourishment along with the spiritual kind? Have a Jewish bake night – and see who comes up with the best Jewish dish. If you want, add a contest element and give a prize for the best dish.

Go on a Mission

There are lots of missions to Israel that offer a religious or spiritual angle. The Great Almighty knows there are enough holy places in the Holy Land to go visit. If your wallet can stretch that far, sign up and see the **Western Wall**, the blue walls of the synagogues in **Safed**, the **Cave of the Patriarchs** in **Hebron**, and the graves of half a dozen *Tzadikim*. And while you're there don't forget to shop for Judaica.

Things You Can Do Today:

1. Subscribe to a Jewish or Israeli newsletter, e-mail list, magazine or weekly paper. These are also often available for free or nearly free at your local Jewish Community Center.
2. Invite an unaffiliated Jew to a synagogue or organization for a prayer or an event.
3. Have people over for a Shabbat meal, with traditional songs and words of Jewish learning.
4. Commit yourself to going to one educational activity each month, whether that means a lecture, a course, or a weekend retreat. The more you know about Judaism, the easier it is to feel a part of the community.
5. Pray at the Western Wall by remote – through **thekotel.org** or **aish.com/wallcam**.
6. Network for business amongst fellow Jews. Mix a little community with that pleasure.
7. If your synagogue doesn't already do it, encourage them to add a prayer for the welfare of the soldiers protecting Israel.
8. Find at least one outreach organization (see resources list) and volunteer your time and/or money.
9. Get involved with your local Jewish Community Center. Tell your unaffiliated friends about their programs and facilities – and then work out together.
10. Volunteer your time at a community school, old age home or vocational service. The latter is a particularly good way to network within the professional world.
11. Think about joining a mission to Israel that will focus on the religious and/or spiritual side of the Holy Land.
12. Have a "Jewish Trivia" night – search the internet for trivia and make your own game of trivial pursuit for your friends.
13. Have a Jewish bake night, and see who comes up with the best of Jewish cooking. If you want, add a contest element and give a prize for the best dish.
14. Organize a Jewish singles event, whether it's a party, a book club meeting, or speed-dating.

12. Strengthening Spiritual Ties to Israel - Christians

I don't think it's an exaggeration to say that without Christian support for Israel, Israel would have a very hard time surviving. And I don't think it's irrelevant in the least that much of that support comes from people who feel a strong spiritual connection to the Holy Land and who believe in the right of the Jews to return to it.

However, even if that support does not come from believing that "He who blesses thee, I will bless; he who curses thee, I will curse" (Genesis 12:3), or from believing that the Jewish return is a precursor to the Second Coming or to the End Times (or other Biblical prophecies), there are ample reasons for Christians to care about Israel, including the fact of it being a democratic society that protects basic freedoms for all its citizens regardless of race or religion. And any strengthening of spiritual feelings towards the Holy Land or about the morality and justice of Israel's existence will, inevitably, help Israel to survive.

A Word About Why Christians Support Israel

On that subject, I feel I should add that this is a book that pre-supposes that the reader already supports Israel – for whatever reason(s). So I don't think it's necessary to delve into the whys – at least when it comes to religion. In particular, as someone who isn't Christian, I don't think it's my place to preach about religious reasons for Christians to support Israel. I have, however, come across a fair number of articles, books, and websites that deal with the issue — so I happily refer anyone who wants more information to peruse the resources list of **Christian Zionism** below and at the back of the book. And, in addition, you may find some organizations on that list that are worth your active support.

That the Jews are connected with God in a special way and that God does not allow that bond to fail is entirely obvious. We wait for the instant in which Israel will say yes to Christ, but we know that it has a special mission in history now... which is significant for the world.
Pope Benedict XVI

Things to Do in Your Church

Connecting spiritually to Israel in church can be as easy as signing up for Bible classes (and paying attention to holy locations) or as time intensive as planning a Christian mission to the country, complete with meetings with Israeli political and religious leaders and visits to Holy sites.

But perhaps the best way for Christians who care about Israel's survival to help would be to work with your own and other churches to actively endorse Israel's right to exist.

I'm not suggesting, of course, that your church has to agree with every policy of any given Israeli government. Heck, no two Jews can agree on any policy undertaken by any particular Israeli administration! In fact, I'm not talking about political statements at all, except in the sense that it's a political statement that the Jewish State has a right to exist at all.

In this day and age, where heads of countries (such as Iran) openly advocate for Israel's demise, it's particularly important to send a message that Israel's right to exist is supported across the globe by non-Jews, especially Christians.

Did You Know?
*Arthur Loomis Harmon, who helped design
the Empire State Building, designed the YMCA
in Jerusalem.*

What this means in practice can vary from small activities by
your church – such as fundraising, investing in Israeli bonds
when you're looking for a place to park some church funds, or
inviting Israeli speakers to your community – to more public
activities, such as broadcasting statements of support (particularly after anti-Semitic statements in the press), including pro-
Israel links and content on your church's website, and actively
working with other Christian groups to negate any hostile
notions about the Jewish State within the Christian world.

It is especially important, I believe, that when some Christian
groups attack the existence of Israel from a theological perspective or from the perspective of ideas of Christian justice, that it
is another Christian church or group that defends Israel. It simply carries more clout – and you have a much better chance of
actually influencing members of those other groups than any
Jew can ever have.

If you want to be proactive about this, then I'd suggest attending Christian groups, camps, conferences and the like and asking them to sign a "declaration of support for Israel" at the end
and then sending that to the press. Even small groups can do
this – it can be surprisingly effective. Remember to send the
press release to local and small newspapers and to put the
declaration on your church's website.

And while this is hardly the place to justify Israel's existence
from the perspective of justice (you may want to check out
christianactionforisrael.org and also look at the list of educational resources at the back of the book), I will point out, briefly,
that Israel is a liberal democracy, with a free press, accords
full citizenship on her minorities (including Arabs), and
allows freedom of worship to all faiths. In stark contrast to
all her neighbors.

Add Website Links

On that note, you might want to lobby your church to add a section to their website about reasons to support the existence of Israel. Check out the resources list below and at the back of the book for ideas. Contact Christian organizations who support the Jewish State and ask for content – or just provide links.

Christian Zionism

SOME ORGANIZATIONS
• Christians United For Israel (www.cufi.org)
• Bridges For Peace (www.bridgesforpeace.com)
• International Christian Embassy Jerusalem (www.icej.org)
• International Christian Zionist Center
  (www.israelmybeloved.com)

ONLINE
• www.patrobertson.com/Speeches/IsraelLauder.asp
• www.christianactionforisrael.org
• www.christian-zionism.org
• www.christiansstandingwithisrael.com
• www.zionismontheweb.org
• www.c4israel.org
• www.cfijerusalem.org
• www.cdn-friends-icej.ca
• www.ifcj.org
• www.pcjcr.org

SOME BOOKS AND MAGAZINES
• Campolo, Tony. "*The Ideological Roots of Christian Zionism.*" Tikkun magazine, January-February 2005.
• Chafets, Zev. *A Match Made in Heaven: American Jews, Christian Zionists, and One Man's Exploration of the Weird and Wonderful Judeo-Evangelical Alliance.* (HarperCollins, 2007).
• Clark,Victoria. *Allies for Armageddon: The Rise of Christian Zionism.* (Yale, 2007).
• Gorenberg, Gershom. *The End of Days: Fundamentalism and the Struggle for the Temple Mount.* (Free Press, 2000).
• Hagee, John. *In Defense of Israel.* (Frontline, 2007).

• Oren, Michael B. Power, *Faith and Fantasy*. (W.W. Norton, 2008).

For more resources check the resources list in the back of the book.

Incorporating the Holy Land into Your Life

It's worth thinking about (or even traveling to) the Holy Land even outside church, too. To start with, it's worth remembering that it's no accident that Israel is called "the Holy Land." When it comes to Holy sites for Christians, Israel rules. This is, after all, the very land in which the events of the Bible took place. What better place to go to truly understand the texts and really feel them?

There is, for instance, **Bethlehem**, city of Jesus' birth and **Golgatha**, site of his crucifixion, as well as the **Church of the Holy Sepulcher** and the **Mount of Olives** and, of course, the **Via Dolorosa** – the very path Jesus walked towards crucifixion, with 13 stations en route. One can visit the city and tunnels under the **Western Wall** and walk on the very streets that existed before the Romans burned the Temple and, up north in the **Galilee**, one can immerse in the same lake that John the Baptist did. Talk about feeling a three dimensional connection to history and religion!

Yet even if it isn't possible to take a physical trip to these Holy sites anytime in the near future, it's still possible to strengthen spiritual connections to them. If you have kids, what better way to get them involved than to have them play games set in Israel? Or perhaps a graphics presentation or virtual experience on the computer? Puzzles, models, games and pictures can be good for classroom activities, too, if your kids belong to a Christian school or after-school group. And if you're feeling particularly creative and energetic, why not make models of Holy sites?

For adults, one can organize (or attend) lecture series about the Holy sites, hang pictures of them on well-viewed walls and desks and take an interest in Biblical archeology. Whether you want to subscribe to magazines such as **Biblical Archeological Review**, go to the library and take out books on the subject or go to museums (Near East section, usually), there are fascinating things happening in archeology that can have a real impact on faith and scholarship (just witness the effect of the **Dead Sea Scrolls**, for instance, found in the **Qumran** caves in the **Judean Desert**).

Other ways of spiritually connecting to the Holy Land can include poring over maps of Israel and identifying which places today correspond to places mentioned in the Bible, finding ancient coins and pottery unearthed in Israel and using them as aids to understanding ordinary living back in Biblical times, and taking virtual tours on the Internet of many Holy locations.

THINGS YOU CAN DO TODAY:

1. Hang pictures of the Holy Land in your house and office. Find photos and e-mail them to your friends and community – frame ones that you like and give them as gifts or park them on your business desk.
2. Plan a trip to the Holy Land, whether on your own or via a mission through your church. Put aside a small amount of money each week for this purpose – in a year or two you could easily have enough to bankroll this. Check out **www.goisrael.com/Tourism_Eng/Tourist+Information/Christian+Themes/Christian+Itineraries.htm** for sample itineraries.
3. Research Holy sites and their archaeology, whether online, at a museum or through a course or lecture series.
4. Dig up (either literally or metaphorically) an ancient coin or oil lamp from Biblical days and display it somewhere prominent in your house, office or church.
5. Take virtual tours of the Holy Land and its Holy sites on the internet.
6. Sign up for a Bible class or two – and study with a map in hand.
7. Teach your kids about Holy places in Israel. Buy maps, books, models and the like – and learn about them together with your children.

8. Pass around a hat or have a bake sale or do other fundraising for Israel or for Christian organizations that support Israel.
9. Invest some church funds in Israeli bonds, paper or stocks.
10. Add a section to your church's website about reasons to support the existence of Israel. Check out the resources list at the back of the book for ideas. Contact Christian organizations who support the Jewish State and ask for content – or provide links.
11. Expand your online network of friends – and e-mail them when you want to send out a public declaration supporting Israel or condemning a bigot. Online petitions, if they garner enough support, can snowball and have a huge effect.
12. Invite Israeli speakers to speak to your church and community.
13. Put out declaratory statements of support for Israel after a leader on the world stage says something very negative or downright anti-Semitic.
14. Teach your kids and your community about the Holocaust as a way of both strengthening tolerance and understanding the need for a Jewish State.
15. Work with other Christian groups who support Israel – and counter the positions of those groups who are hostile.
16. Attend Christian groups, camps, conferences and the like and ask them to sign a "declaration of support for Israel" at the end and then send that to the press. Even small groups can do this. Remember to send the press release to local and small newspapers and to put the declaration on your church's website.
17. Ask your church to approach Jewish organizations and synagogues in the area and see where they can cooperate on issues relating to Israel.

PART 7

THE NEXT GENERATION

13. A Word about Educating our Children

It's entirely possible to be a stalwart defender of Israel even if you've never had a stitch of formal education about the country itself, Jewish history, culture or religion.

Indeed, you may have had a particularly negative experience with Jewish education as a kid, and *still* want to see Israel defended, body and soul.

And yet, it stands to reason that the more we know about a subject the more effective we will be at analyzing its issues, weighing arguments, and coming to reasonable conclusions. Education, whether spoon-fed to us in formal classes or acquired on our own, is highly valuable.

And what's true for us is doubly true for our kids. After all, if you want to predict the future, just look at your kids and their friends. 100 years from now it will be their children and grandchildren who will be running the show. It will be *their* decisions regarding Israel that will help determine Israel's continued viability.

It seems to me, then, that the most important thing that we, as people who care about Israel, can do is make sure that our kids care too, and with as much passion and dedication, if not more, that we feel ourselves. And that the simplest, most effective, way to ensure this is through educating our children about the country and about its history, identity, culture, and religion – whether we send them to schools who teach them these subjects formally or whether we undertake to teach them the necessities on our own.

I. INFORMAL EDUCATION: BEYOND SCHOOL

Never let school get in the way of your education. That's what my father, quoting Mark Twain, always said to me (and he was a principal!) – and it still holds true. Our best education comes after classroom hours are over.

So here are some ideas to help your kids educationally connect to Israel even if their school won't lift a thumb.

Talk at Dinner

People talk about things that they care about. If you're not talking about anything related to Israel almost ever – then your kids are getting the clear message that Israel is not worth very much to you.

There are plenty of things that relate to Israel to discuss, even in passing. Almost no country gets as much press, and there are online groups, newspapers, books and blogs from which to find fodder for dinner conversations. Try to read at least one thing about Israel every day. And then look for a way to bring it up, at least for a few minutes.

Better yet, give each of your kids a small assignment – to find one Israel-related topic to bring to the table. You can even have an award for the "best topic of the week" to add extra motivation.

Send Them to Community Events

Wherever you live, it's a sure bet that your community holds at least a few events over the course of the year that can spark a connection between your children and the Jewish State. Whether it's a parade for **Israel's Independence Day**, a service for **Holocaust Memorial Day**, a walk-a-thon or other fundraiser, or just a local speaker talking about current events in the Middle East, there are ways to join with the rest of the community that involve, at least peripherally, Israel. Find the events that are the least boring – and take your kids.

Organize Family Educational Outings

Here's an idea that doesn't require you to wait until the community organizes something: take your family on fun outings that are also educational.

Sometimes these are no-brainers, like trips to a Jewish museum or to the Near Eastern sections of a general museum. Or to a concert with an Israeli band playing (taking their Hebrew out for a spin). Other times, you'll have to bring the education part with you. A trip to the zoo, for instance, could be an opportunity to discuss what kind of animals live in the Holy Land – and their adaptability to Israel's geography (did you know that leopards live in the Negev desert? Or that the lion is Jerusalem's symbol?). A little research online before your outing can go a long way.

Other ideas for educational outings can include trips to City Hall (a chance to compare the local system to Israel's), to the Israeli Consulate (if you've arranged it in advance) or even, albeit it's a bit of a stretch – to the mall. Why the mall? Because you can make a game of trying to discover how many obviously Israeli brand names are represented in any given store – a lesson in world trade! (And, of course, assuming your kid is the right age, this has the advantage of also distracting him or her long enough for you to shop too).

As usual, only our imaginations limit us in bringing an awareness of Israel into even the most ordinary parts of our children's lives.

Top Ten Ways to Help Israel Together with Your Children:

1. Ask your kids to find an article about Israel online and bring it up for discussion at dinner.
2. Do a puzzle with an Israeli theme (a map of Israel, an Israeli painting or the like).
3. Take them to an Israel Day parade, if there's one in your city.
4. Write a letter together to an Israeli soldier (see Chapter 15 for details).
5. Prepare an Israeli food dish together.
6. Watch an Israeli video or film.
7. Create a calendar, t-shirt, or other useful stuff with Israeli pictures.
8. Buy or create jewelry with an Israeli style or theme.
9. Give your children some coins to drop into an Israel-related charity box once a week. Every few months, roll the coins together.
10. Create crosswords together, with the questions about Israel.

Bring Israeli Food into Your Home

In a similar vein, the simple act of just cooking or buying typical Israeli foods can spark a conversation or interest by your kids in other things Israeli. And if you hate to cook, go to an Israeli restaurant and maybe you can even make a friend or two while you're there.

Have a Family Song-fest, Israel-style

If the weather will accommodate it, make a bonfire (find a local park that allows it), and bring your family and friends – then bring Israeli songs along to sing or listen to while you're roasting marshmallows.

Watch Israeli TV

If you'd rather stay indoors, then you can try to watch Israeli TV (via satellite, cable or the internet) as a family and educational event. Whether it's talking about the news or comparing Israeli movies to American or British ones, this is an easy-to-plan and easy-to-implement idea.

Have Israel-themed Birthday Parties

They come once a year for each of your children and their friends, and you know that a party comes with them. So why not buy Israeli food, dress up in blue and white, hand out Israeli chocolates and play Israeli music for their birthdays? And if you want to get more educational, screen an Israeli documentary, talk about current events or dramatic historical events, have the kids re-enact various Israeli battles, or put on a play. Just don't forget to dress the cake in blue and white icing!

Make a Weekly Ritual of Giving Charity

Dropping a few coins in an Israel-related charity box together with your children can be a meaningful experience for both you and your children. Making this a once-a-week ritual ensures that your children have a connection to Israel that also reminds them of home, something they'll remember for decades to come. And every few months, you can have another activity – rolling the coins together and adding them up.

Find (or Start) a Youth Group

A youth group is probably the best thing for kids if there's a local one you can find that you like. It has it all: social aspects, educational aspects, and time away from a screen!

Check out the resources list for examples of youth groups that already exist. And if there are none that you like – consider starting your own! It doesn't have to be so hard – just find a few local kids near the ages of your own and hire a college student who isn't a dork but who does know something about Israel to plan a few activities. Ideas for activities? Anything from a simple pizza night with an Israeli film to a trip to a local museum to a night around a bonfire listening to cool or funny stories (perhaps from people who've recently visited Israel). The trick here, by the way, is to get the other parents involved first – and then you drag the kids into it. Then get their feedback, but don't forget that some kids like to complain.

Send Them to Summer Camp

It can be expensive or cheap depending on the camp (and, like the youth group idea, you may want to start your own, if you have the energy), but summer camp is almost always both educational and fun. It also carries with it built-in benefits of keeping your kids active and making sure they make friends with others who share at least some of your values.

Once again, check out the resources list for some ideas. And don't forget that there are some foundations or companies who are willing to sponsor a local child to go to camp (for example, check out **www.jewishcamping.org**). Creativity helps in the money department – perhaps you can persuade a local business that it's worth it to underwrite your child's camp experience in return for the camp buying or advertising some of the business's products. Then approach the camp and pitch them that business's products or ad campaign. You might, for example, convince the local optician to pay for tuition in return for the camp agreeing to refer any kid with broken glasses to them for the duration of the summer (especially if the optician offers a discount). Or perhaps the local candy store would be interested in donating the money for the whole camp to wear t-shirts with their slogan – and would be willing to cough up a few more greenbacks to include your kid's entrance fee, since you're the one setting the whole thing up.

Set Up a Private Class

If your child's school doesn't have the Israel-oriented courses you want, you may want to get together with a few other parents (or just on your own) and give your kids some private projects to work on. This can be anything from having a formal tutor who gives out homework and checks to see that they do it to making sure that your kids just read the headlines of an Israeli newspaper each day.

The trick with any private class or tutoring is to make it part of your child's routine. In cannot be ad hoc or it won't work. Even if it's only ten minutes a day, make sure it's the same ten minutes – and right after they come home from school is probably best.

Have a Mock Debate

If you want your kids to learn about politics (Israeli, global or local) then you might want to consider running a mock **UN** or other debate about Israeli politics, with you as the referee. To do this properly, have your kids each choose a side of an argument (for example Israel vs. Iran) and have them research their side online. Then have a formal debate: each side having a five minute chance to present their side and then responding to questions. Then you award some prize for the winner (not on content but on presentation). If your kids have an interest, this could be not just educational but fun.

II. FORMAL EDUCATION – TEACHING ISRAEL AT SCHOOL

There are plenty of opportunities to teach about Israel in a school setting, whether you send your kids to private school or public. Israel is a Western, democratic country in a highly important region of the world, with enormous amounts of drama surrounding both its past and its present. The simple truth is that schools *ought* to be talking about Israel, whether we push for it or not. But "ought to be doing" and "actually doing" are different beasts – and it's up to us to get involved, for the sake of our kids' values.

A) BEEF-UP ISRAEL-RELATED PROGRAMS IN PRIVATE SCHOOLS

Whether it's a Jewish school or a Christian one, there are plenty of Israel-related programs and studies that ought to be encouraged, outside of the obvious religious-oriented ones.

For example, we might want to start by learning how to communicate with Israelis directly – by studying Hebrew.

Teaching Hebrew

In a Jewish school, there's simply no excuse not to teach at least the basics of Hebrew. And in non-Jewish schools there are plenty of benefits too. Besides the ability to read the Bible in its original script, the simple learning of a foreign language brings an awareness of different ways of thinking and tackling problems. This can only help broaden our kids' minds. Incidentally, this is a great time to be thinking about hiring an Israeli teacher and have the students relate to a person who can answer questions all year long about the conflicts in the Middle East.

And besides, it would really help them find their way to the nearest bathroom if they ever go and visit the place. Which brings us to a great idea – a class trip.

Plan a School Trip to Israel

It's a little out of the way for most class trips, but if you can find a way of subsidizing it, there's really nothing as helpful as a trip to Israel to cement an emotional attachment to the country. Visit the Holy sites, bring history to life, and meet fascinating people. What's not to like?

Okay, so there are a few little bumps in the road about financing this, insurance etc. This is a great time to get creative and find solutions that will also get the kids involved. How about a car wash run by the students? How about a bake-a-thon (admission NOT free) with a prize for the best recipe? What about holding a few raffles, with prizes donated by local businesses? Or finding one or more corporate sponsors to underwrite some expenses?

> *"Tis education forms the common mind, Just as the twig is bent, the tree's inclined."*
> **-Alexander Pope.**

If planning a trip for the whole class seems too daunting, maybe it makes sense to start smaller – with only a handful of students chosen to go each year with one teacher (maybe that Israeli who was hired to teach Hebrew...). The sheer competition for the privilege of going could generate real excitement and interest in all things Israeli. The school could run an essay contest – with the top five entries winning the trip. Or perhaps the best website design that promotes interest in the Jewish State. Or maybe the most innovative way to make Israeli history exciting to ADD teens, or even the most compelling reason a particular Israeli film does or does not deserve an Oscar. Truly, the list of potential ideas is endless.

Teaching Israeli Subjects – Create Modules

If we want our children to be intellectually aware of subjects concerning Israel then we need to include courses in Israeli history, geography, and economics in our schools. Since full-fledged courses are a tough sell, an equally viable idea is the mini-course, or the module: a micro-course wedged into a larger course. These mini-courses could include a strategy module, focusing on how small countries like Israel survive (perhaps as part of a course on small countries in Europe and Asia), a military history course which could analyze both Israeli victories like the **Six Day War** and failures such as the **2006 Second Lebanon** War, or a conservation course, focusing on issues relating to conserving water and environmental resources in Israel and its surrounding countries – a particularly interesting subject considering these countries often have no relationship with each other or a very frosty one at best.

Foster Social Connections to Israelis

This is one that can initially start out as a homework project but could then continue on its own. Assign a class to troll the Internet, find Israeli students their age and start up a conversation – about anything, from music to politics. Many Israelis are proficient enough in English to carry on these kinds of conversations; or it could be a project for the Hebrew classes.

Appoint yourself a teacher and acquire
for yourself a study partner.
Ethics of our Fathers (Pirkei Avot) 1:6

Create an "Israel Day"

Have an "Israel Day" at school, where all the teachers include at least a few references to Israel in the course of their regular teaching. Decorate the school in blue and white, drape Israeli flags over the windows, serve falafel and Israeli salad, hire a band to play Israeli music, screen an Israeli film, and maybe even schedule an Israeli speaker or a debate. Israel's **Independence Day** could be an obvious good date to work around.

Create Textbooks or Materials

Private schools have a good deal of control over which textbooks to use – and everyone ought to be looking through each subject's textbook to see if there is anything offensive in them. But while we're looking, maybe we can suggest to the author(s) that they include some references to Israel or examples of Israeli contributions to their field for the next edition of their books.

And even if we can't – we can always create supplemental materials in many subjects that can shine a positive light on Israel's contributions. Some perfect examples of this would be to discuss **Teva**, an Israeli pharmaceutical company, in context of discussing generic drugs and patents; discussing Israeli hi-tech firms such as **Checkpoint**, as part of a business course or computer course; or debating **Israel's Supreme Court** decisions regarding torture.

Of course, in any religious courses it should be obvious that there are great opportunities to highlight Israeli connections to religion. This is the Holy Land we're discussing, after all and its connection to Judaism, Christianity and Islam is plain for all to explore.

Invite Israeli Guest Speakers

Plenty of teachers would probably jump at the chance to have a guest expert teach their classes for a period or two. Contact the Israeli Consulate or go online to find local Israeli businesses and ask around to see if there is anyone who fits the bill for any particular class.

B) TALKING ABOUT ISRAEL IN PUBLIC SCHOOLS

It's much harder to convince a public school to talk about Israel (and certainly regarding any of the religious parts, such as the connection of the land to the Bible). But parents can still push to have Israel brought into the discussions in any given class. Meet with teachers, preferably outside of just school events, and sound them out about their receptiveness to including mini-courses in their classrooms or as part of extra credit. Suggest books to the English department teachers, films and music to the arts program directors and offer to set up and pay for guest speakers. Since Israel is often in the news, offer to have debates on current events and the Middle East. Also, although not strict-ly about Israel, push to have the **Holocaust** taught about – this is important in and of itself, and helps students identify with the need for Jews to have a secure homeland.

In short, many of the same ideas from above, modified for a public school, can be utilized.

Sending Jewish Kids to Jewish Schools

Not everyone will agree with me on this, I know, but I believe that the simplest, best, and most viable way to ensure that Jewish kids in the Diaspora have an emotional and intellectual connection to Israel by the time they turn 18 is to send them to a Jewish school (whether a full day school or a part time Sunday school) and for that school to have strong Israel-related programs.

In addition to whatever formal learning they'll acquire, they'll also develop lasting social connections within the community, a deeper religious experience and a far better feel for the rhythm of the Jewish calendar.

That said, what if you just can't afford to do this? While many communities have found ways to subsidize or otherwise obtain funding for Jewish schools, many haven't. For some of my own thoughts on this subject, please see the addendum to this chapter, after the **Things You Can Do Today** section.

THINGS YOU CAN DO TODAY:

1. Bring up one topic each day about Israel over dinner. Read newspapers and blogs for ideas to spark good conversations. Or ask your kids to each find a topic to bring up. Turn this into a game.
2. Bring Israeli food into your home – and talk about it.
3. Take your family to an Israeli restaurant.
4. Watch Israeli TV (via satellite, cable or the internet) as a family event.
5. Make a bonfire. Bring your family and friends – then bring Israeli songs along to sing or listen to while you're roasting marshmallows.
6. Get your kids talking to Israelis online.
7. Look out for community events that your kids will enjoy.
8. Organize educational outings that are also fun. Invite your kids' friends to come along.
9. Have Israel-themed birthday parties and give Israeli gifts.

10. Find or start a youth group for your children.
11. Send your kids to camp. (Or start one yourself.)
12. Arrange for a private teacher (maybe a college student) to teach your kids and/or a number of families.
13. Suggest that the school hold a competition for a trip to Israel. The best kinds of competition should involve the students – and motivate them to learn something they otherwise wouldn't.
14. Plan a school trip to Israel. Talk to the school and your kids about creative and fun ways to fundraise.
15. Suggest courses and mini-courses that touch upon Israel-oriented subjects and could be taught within the current curriculum.
16. Push for classes in school that teach Hebrew. Maybe go to one yourself, with or without your children.
17. Create textbooks or materials that teach about Israel.
18. Create an "Israel Day" at the school.
19. Invite Israelis to speak at the school.
20. Make sure the school teaches about the Holocaust.
21. Decide to make it your goal, if you have a Jewish child, to send him or her to a Jewish day school or Sunday school.

ADDENDUM

A Few Thoughts about Paying for Jewish Day School Tuition

The sad truth is that as tuition prices skyrocket in private Jewish day schools, many parents who desperately want to send their children to Jewish schools are being effectively forced out of the day schools, at least in some communities. So what do you do if you're a parent in one of these places and you want in?

Quite simply, I believe that we must, as parents and as a community, come up with money for the next generation – and we need to be as creative as possible about it because many parents just can't afford full tuition, even without multiple kids in the system.

Tuition is a Community Problem

So, here is the first thing I suggest: We need to decide that our goal, on a community by community basis, is to have Jewish day school education within reach of every Jewish family that wants it.

Since that goal is far easier said than done, we will undoubtedly need to conduct ongoing community-wide meetings to figure out how to get there. We need day school principals to explain their budgets to the community in real detail. Transparency is key. The more information transmitted to the community, the more likely it is that the community can find creative solutions.

Secondly, we need to recruit more volunteers. We are living in a world with more students learning in full-time yeshivas than in any other period of history – yet there is a shortage of Jewish teachers. Let's marry these two communities off. If the heads of the yeshivas can be persuaded to add a community-service portion to their yeshiva's schedule (however modest), then perhaps each Jewish school could be running a high-quality Jewish education program without the corresponding high costs. In addition, post-army Israelis interested in spending a year or two abroad should be recruited for these tasks too. This would both expose the students to real Israelis, often close to their age, and would be potentially cheaper than recruiting new teachers – especially if members of the community offered to host the teachers for a year at a time.

In addition, we need to make it de rigueur for members of the community to leave in their wills a small percentage of their estate to further Jewish education. What could be more fitting than for the generation leaving this earth to help sustain the education of those just coming into it? (There are many who embrace this approach, incidentally, including George Hanus of Chicago, who launched a campaign he called "**Operation Jewish Education/ The 5 Percent Answer.**")

There are many other ways to fundraise for education – from the classic telemarketers' techniques to creative requests from government sources. Let's pool our heads together at regular community meetings and solve this problem.

And on the note of creative ways to solve this issue, here's a radical idea that I'd like to propose: a Jewish Student Loan Association modeled on the U.S. government's student loan programs ("Sallie Mae"). It can work as follows:

"Jellie Mae"

Whether we organize it as a global endeavor, a national company, or whether each community works it out for itself, the idea is straightforward: finance Jewish education over the course of a Jewish child's whole career.

A Jewish education lasts a lifetime – but is paid for, currently, at high costs for 12 years. It would be far more sensible to loan the money for tuition to each student (or his/her parents) and have the student (or parents) pay it back over the course of a long working lifetime.

Call it "Jellie Mae," as a "Jewish Loan" riff on Sallie Mae.

Jellie Mae would be a special kind of loan, where parents would participate in the application process and where the money could be paid directly to qualified Jewish schools. Ideally, these loans would not need collateral and would only start to accumulate interest when the child hits 18. Better yet, have a grace period where students wouldn't need to begin paying it off until they hit 25, or have been working for at least a year.

While there may be some objection to burdening a child with financial obligations of this sort, the reality is that for most students the payments would be reasonable – probably less than the student loan payments from college – and if Jewish education is important, then this is worth it. (Of course, legally it would probably still be the parents on the hook, and no doubt many students might want to insist that the parents be the ones to shoulder the obligation, but this would still be an easier burden on parents than the current system).

In addition, it would be desirable to have an option for students to apply to have their payments reduced, suspended or even forgiven if they move to Israel or work in Jewish community service, to encourage these things.

So how do we finance Jellie Mae? There are many options, but here are a few ideas to start: create a company which would sell shares and would use the money from these shares to finance the loans initially. Eventually, of course, as students/parents pay back the loans the program should become self-sustaining and even profitable.

Ideally, shares in Jellie Mae could eventually become a sensible part of financial portfolios even without caring about its purpose.

To kick-start the program, I would suggest that we take 5% of the money that gets transferred annually by federations to various charities and organizations in Israel – and have the federations invest that money on behalf of the charities in shares of Jellie Mae (either a national company, or a local equivalent). That is, for every $100 that the community would send to, say, the **Jewish Agency** in Israel, send $95 and buy, on their behalf, $5 worth of shares in Jellie Mae. The charity loses a small part of operating cash but gains an investment that is financially viable and helps Jewish education.

Thirty years down the road, the shares will bring better returns and the students who otherwise would not have received a Jewish education will be more connected to the community and to Israel. This is truly a win-win scenario.

PART 8

BATTLES TO BE FOUGHT

14. Fighting anti-Israel Forms of anti-Semitism

Entire tomes have been written on anti-Semitism, but for our purposes (that is, in the context of helping Israel continue to survive) it should suffice to say that, in general, the less anti-Semitism there is in the world, the safer Israel will be; and that there is a specific form of anti-Semitism which people who care about Israel should be particularly vigilant about and that is the trend today for those who hate the Jews to disguise this hatred as merely being against the State of Israel.

> *Criticizing Israel is not anti-Semitic, and saying so is vile. But singling out Israel for opprobrium and international sanction – out of all proportion to any other party in the Middle East – is anti-Semitic, and not saying so is dishonest.*
> **Thomas Friedman (New York Times)**

I. IDENTIFYING ANTI-SEMITISM

When it comes to anti-Israel statements or policies it's not always obvious whether anti-Semitism is involved or whether the statement or policy is merely a criticism (valid or otherwise) of an Israeli policy. So here a few easy ways of identifying anti-Semitic statements or campaigns regarding Israel:

- They attack the existence of Israel; that is, the only way to solve their grievance is to *destroy* the Jewish State.
- They apply clear double standards: one for Israel, another for every other country in the world. Similarly, they deceptively and disproportionately single Israel out in a list of offenders – usually with the goal of "punishing" Israel in some way (a boycott or exclusion from a world body being good examples). It's useful to remember that even respected world bodies, such as the UN, can be (and have been) manipulated, by those seeking to destroy Israel, to pass resolutions and declarations that are then employed by campaigns to attack Israel.
- They use classic anti-Semitic methods and imagery (accusations that Israelis are poisoning Arab candy or water sources and cartoon images of IDF soldiers devouring Palestinian children are obvious examples; accusing the Jews and/or Israel of "controlling" the world or the media (or being "behind" every tragedy, including the 9/11 attacks) is another).
- They seek to "tone down" the Holocaust, whether by denying it outright, downplaying it, or saying that the Israelis today are "just as bad".

Often, people will accept that Israel ought to be criticized for some policy or another – and are thus reluctant, despite the anti-Semitism, to get involved in a counter campaign. The solution, I think, is to clearly state your criticism – but then fight the anti-Semitic campaign. There are legitimate forums for criticism; campaigns seeking to hurt or destroy Israel are not one of them.

Of course, when it comes to more general forms of anti-Semitism, including those without any mention of Israel specifically, it is also crucial that we identify both the statements and those who are spreading them.

II. PREVENTING ANTI-SEMITISM

The Importance of Education

An ounce of prevention beats a pound of cure and when it comes to anti-Semitism that couldn't be truer. Whether it's classic anti-Semitism or the newest forms of anti-Semitism, teaching our kids why it's wrong is a necessity if we want to fight it in the long term.

Teaching Tolerance at Home

Whether it's by interacting with members of other communities and faiths or by studying each other's cultures, teaching tolerance is the key to defeating anti-Semitism. Kids are very quick to pick up when parents don't like other faiths or races. Don't leave tolerance-teaching to the schools. Start at home, by bringing other people to the dinner table, films to be watched and books to be read. And don't think your kids don't notice what language you use when you're angry.

Holocaust Education

Often the quickest and most visual way of demonstrating where anti-Semitism can lead, books and films about the Holocaust abound. If your local schools don't already teach this, hound them about it. And if they do, don't stop there: talk about it at home, watch **Schindler's List** with your kids, invite a survivor to speak to your community, visit a museum – in short, do whatever it takes to make it real for anyone who doesn't know about it. This isn't, of course, fun. It is, however, important.

Teaching the History and Politics of Judaism and Israel

Understanding Israel's history and its politics is important for anyone who wants to combat anti-Semitism, if only because the two have become so intertwined. Regardless of where you stand on any present issue, propaganda is so heavily disseminated on these topics that it's important to know what is true and what is not. Although some schools may teach this, I'd suggest getting involved in this area yourself, if you want your kids to be truly knowledgeable. Once again, books, films and the internet are great resources. Don't forget your local library and community courses.

And while you're at it, you may want to know something about Judaism in general and the history of the Jews and of anti-Semitism throughout the ages. It's an unfortunate truth that history here repeats itself all too often.

Although this subject can be overwhelming, I'd suggest spending about 15 minutes twice a week or perhaps ten minutes each day, for a few months, to get a good feel for this. To make this more fun, choose a friend and learn together. Or perhaps each of you can learn different things and then compare notes at the end of the week. If you want some competitive juices to flow, perhaps suggest that the person who comes up with the most interesting fact gets treated to coffee by the other.

If Algeria introduced a resolution declaring that the earth was flat and that Israel had flattened it, it would pass by a vote of 164 to 13 with 26 abstentions.
Abba Eban

On College Campuses

While I won't repeat here the advice from previous chapters (see the chapters **Becoming a Spokesperson for Israel** and **Helping Israel on Campus: The College Years**, and note that much of the advice will apply regarding anti-Semitism too), it's worth noting that the college campus should be the first place we look at when it comes to charting attitudes towards Jews in our general society. What is extreme on campus becomes mainstream in society, within a relatively short span of time, if left unchallenged. College students have a disproportionate responsibility to be aware of anti-Semitism, in all its forms, and to speak up when they see and hear it – especially from people who are "normal." And parents and faculty (and donors) have a real responsibility to pay close attention too. Check the resources list at the back of the book for websites and books that specialize in both providing information and assistance.

III. COMBATTING ANTI-SEMITISM

Speaking with One Voice

The first line of defense in attacking anti-Semitism directly is to rally our forces. In addition, as this is a long-term battle, it is important to have our forces unified (or able to be rallied) on a long-term basis.

What this means in practice is that we must learn to agree to disagree on all kinds of issues and politics but unite when it comes to the issues of anti-Semitism and Israel's basic legitimacy. This is as true within our respective communities as it is between our communities. We must marginalize our extremists when it comes to these issues and strive to be aware of how our own opinions and statements are perceived by those who wish Israel ill. We must, in short, speak with one voice on these topics.

Speaking Up

The easiest thing in the world is to let a co-worker or friend say something anti-Semitic and just let it go. They're often nice people, after all, and many times don't even realize that what they're saying may be offensive. Not to mention that occasionally you run into someone quite dumb. (I worked with someone once, for example, who was convinced that Jews had horns. When I pointed out that I don't have any – he said that "real Jews" do and I must not be one of them!) You don't have to rake someone over the coals when they say something offensive, but you should speak up.

Fighting Online

It's equally important, in this day and age, to be trolling the internet and blogging your comments when someone says something anti-Semitic online. In addition, it pays to belong to or support groups who keep honest records of history, dispel myths, and take note of creeping racism, especially on mainstream websites.

Understanding that Jews Can Be Touchy

Jews have a long history of being persecuted and an all too recent experience of seeing how anti-Jewish behavior can escalate from words to violence with terrible ferocity. So it ought to be understandable that Jews react with a high degree of sensitivity when someone says something that can be perceived as anti-Semitic. It also ought to be understandable that other people, without this Jewish experience, might think that Jews are overreacting. When reacting to things that may be anti-Semitic bear in mind that we all have different experiences. For Jews this means we should be careful not to jump too quickly to label someone an anti-Semite. For non-Jews this means remembering that sometimes Jews are quicker to recognize anti-Semitism due to long experience.

> *Europe is reawakening its old demons, but today there is a difference. The old anti-Semitism and anti-Zionism have morphed into something more dangerous.*
> **Denis MacShane, co-chair of a British parliamentary inquiry which reported on anti-Semitism in the UK in September 2006.**

Creating Committees

One way of uniting members of our communities who don't normally interact is to create ad-hoc committees and standing committees to deal with anti-Semitism within our community. If your community already has one or more committee in place that regularly reacts to anti-Semitic statements and issues, consider joining it or volunteering to help out with its work. If your community (or government, for that matter) doesn't have these already – create one. Gather together a few community leaders (businesspeople, rabbis, priests, principals, lawyers, and other professionals) and hold a meeting at which you ask people to join your committee and meet once every 3 months to discuss ways of fighting any anti-racial and anti-Semitic tendencies that are present in your community. Network with other groups fighting discrimination and then if and when someone says or does something inflammatory, issue a statement together. When a community (and its politicians) sees that its leadership is condemning anti-Semitism it really does send a message.

Striking Fear into the Hearts of Anti-Semites

It's important that those who are deliberately spewing their hatred of the Jews understand that there are consequences to this. I'm not advocating violence here – merely the notion that all of society should band together and shun those who would advocate for a race's destruction. It should be harder for anti-Semites to get jobs, join the PTA, and assume community leadership positions. It should be obvious that, given the choice, we choose to take our money and business to their competitors. In short, they should know that society is watching and reacting, and not silently allowing anti-Semitism to continue.

Measuring Progress

On a similar note, where a crime is committed that has anti-Semitism as a material component, we should be taking note of it. Police forces should be tracking this data, reporting it to political bodies, and making it public. It's important to have mechanisms to measure our success in fighting anti-Semitism, especially the most egregious parts of it: actual acts of vandalism and violence.

It's important, therefore, that we press our local police force to keep records of anti-Semitic and other racial crimes and to measure the community's progress in fighting them. In addition, we should be asking our elected representatives to keep track of anti-Semitism and issue an annual report on the topic.

A Few Key Resources:

· *The Anti Defamation League (ADL), dedicated to fighting intolerance, at www.adl.org.*
· *The Simon Wiesenthal Center, for understanding and teaching the Holocaust, at www.wiesenthal.com.*
· *www.eyeontheun.org, to track the UN.*
For more resources check the resources list in the back of the book.

Fighting Anti-Semitism in NGO's and World Bodies

It's especially important to speak up loudly when it's an otherwise respectable institution or organization that is spouting or silently acquiescing to anti-Semitism. Whether it's the **UN** or famous Non Governmental Organizations (NGO's), when anti-Semitism appears (usually in the form of blatant, disproportionate, discrimination against Israel) we must speak up, talk to the people in charge, expose them in the media, and threaten the organization's funding. It's important, too, to press for strict rules prohibiting racism and anti-Semitism as prerequisites within any organization that we or our governments fund.

Specifically, I suggest that we ask any charity or NGO that we support whether they have any rules in place prohibiting them from partaking in anti-Semitic forums or sponsoring anti-Semitic declarations. If they don't, we should press them to adopt a variation of such a rule. Similarly, we ought to press our elected representatives to block government funding for any organization that endorses or espouses anti-Semitism.

Thus, when the **UN's Human Rights Council** has members of the most repressive regimes sitting and singling out Israel for condemnation, it's not just a farce – it ought to be cause for a review of any organization that relies on this council's findings or cites it favorably in its literature. We must "name and shame" not just the HRC, but its supporters and financiers.

To keep up to date on these issues, check out **www.eyeonthe-un.org**, **www.ngo-monitor.org**, and **www.unwatch.org**.

THINGS YOU CAN DO TODAY:

1. Decide to spend 10 minutes a day for a week, learning the history of the Jews, of anti-Semitism, or of present-day Israel. At the end of the week, talk about what you've learned to someone at work or to your family or friends.
2. Learn how to distinguish between honest criticism of Israeli policies and anti-Semitism.
3. Say something nice about Jews to a colleague or friend. Mention some hi-tech achievement by an Israeli company.
4. Speak up (politely) when someone says something offensive to Jews or Israel, especially if they don't realize that they may be offending.
5. Respond to anti-Semitic blogs and websites.
6. Work with people you normally disagree with when it comes to speaking out against instances of anti-Semitism.
7. Talk to the extremists that you are aware of. Try to make a difference.
8. Educate your kids: give them books, movies, and tapes regarding other cultures and especially Jews. Teach tolerance at home.
9. Watch **Schindler's List**. Or any Holocaust documentary.
10. If you're the victim of an anti-Semitic incident, report it.
11. Interact with members of other faiths (see the chapter **Improving Relations Between Jews and Non-Jews**) and talk to them about Israel and Jews in general.
12. Shun those people that you know are spouting anti-Semitism. Avoid their stores, refuse their invitations and don't offer them a platform to spout their venom further.
13. Invite a Holocaust survivor to speak at a public event or on campus.
14. Ask whatever charity or NGO you support whether they have any rules in place prohibiting them from partaking in anti-Semitic forums or sponsoring anti-Semitic declarations. If they don't, press them to adopt a variation of such a rule.

15. Create committees. Lots of them:
    interfaith, inter-organizational, neighborhood committees,
    online groups, the works. Then discuss local and global
    anti-Semitism and brainstorm how to combat it.
16. Press the local police to keep records of anti-Semitic and
    other racial crimes and to measure the community's
    progress in fighting them.
17. Ask your elected representatives to keep track of anti-
    Semitism and issue an annual report on the topic.
18. Press elected representatives to not allow government
    funding for an organization that endorses or espouses
    anti-Semitism.
19. Name and shame those countries, NGOs, and world bodies
    that allow anti-Semitism (for example, the **Human Rights
    Council**) and ask your local media to expose them and their
    financial supporters.

15. Helping Israel in Times of War

When Israel goes to war, the whole country pulls together. For once, the intense political debates subside, the petty squabbles are put aside – and everyone tries to pitch in to help. Whether it's a corporation that donates cell phones to soldiers, a bank that stays open despite attacks, or individuals who provide food and shelter to complete strangers, helping is the watchword of the hour.

Fact is, it's seldom more crucial to support Israel than when the country is actively at war. Although from a strictly military perspective there may be little that someone living outside Israel can contribute, there is still a great deal of essential work that pro-Israel supporters can undertake during periods of war, especially when it comes to morale and propaganda.

Countering Propaganda

Public relations have become an important part of today's military battlefield. Real-time reporting and instant global communications have changed how we view conflicts and the political outcome of a battle may be dramatically different depending not just on what actually happened on the field but on how those battles are perceived by the world. For a country as small and as dependant on the rest of the world as Israel, keeping the media and respectable internet sites honest is as crucial a part of the war as the actual fighting.

Which means, simply, that we must speak up when we see bias, not to mention downright fraud. Whether it's a news station, a website, or a politician being careless with essential facts, we must make our voices heard. We must write letters and e-mails to the press, expose lies circulating in the blogs and stay on top of easy-to-miss fake photos and stories that will inevitably surface.

Don't assume that small stories that are inaccurate are not important. And don't assume that just because the press is swamped with e-mails that no-one will care if there's one more. Every voice counts and every fraudulent accusation has the potential to go down as history if left unchallenged.

If you do spot a fraudulent story, be sure to tell organizations such as the **ADL (Anti Defamation League)**, other members of the press, and websites such as **www.camera.org** and **honestreporting.com**, which track the media.

Expressing Our Support

Besides speaking up when we see an outright lie, it's important that we talk to our local and national elected representatives and tell them that we support Israel – and are noticing if *they* do. Politicians benefit from this conversation because they generally need ammunition in the form of future votes to have the courage to act.

Whether it's in the form of a letter, an e-mail, a phone call or a telegram, be sure to ask your government, at all levels, to support Israel.

Flying an Israeli Flag

Yet another way to publicly express our support – and a very easy one at that – is to fly Israel's blue and white flag from our cars, homes, offices, synagogues, and churches. (You can also get buttons and lapels with a flag on them). If you don't own and/or can't find an Israeli flag, consider making one yourself:

take a white billboard and draw two horizontal blue lines and a Star of David between them. It doesn't have to be perfect.

Using Bumper Stickers

Your car is seen by many strangers. Consider putting an "I Support Israel" or other pro-Israel bumper stickers on your car.

Cutting off Funding for Israel's Enemies

Support all legal efforts to shut down charities that are nothing but front groups for terrorist organizations. Ask your politicians what progress has been made in this area and press for details so that you know which charities to be wary of.

While you're at it, consider the idea of using less oil and gas, since a portion of every dollar at the pump finds its way back to countries still at war with the Jewish State.

Donating Money to Israel

In addition to all the ideas elsewhere in this book, when Israel is at war you may want to concentrate on charities that will help Israel's war efforts. Good examples are the **Magen David Adom**, **LIBI**, and charities for civilian victims (see the resources list at the end of the book and the partial list in this chapter). In addition, Jewish organizations around the world are sure to be running special campaigns to help the war effort or recovery.

You might also want to ask other people to give to these charities as their "gift" to you for your special occasions, instead of a regular present.

Sending a Letter or Package to an Israeli Soldier

Sometimes a personal letter is the best boost to a soldier's morale. If you don't know any soldiers yourself, you may be able to connect with one through the **Jewish Agency**. Try using e-mail, to start: send a letter as an attachment to an e-mail to:

LetterToSoldier@jazo.org.il. The Jewish Agency in Jerusalem will (hopefully) place the letter into an envelope and see that it is delivered to a soldier. If you'd rather use snail mail, send your letter to: Letter for an Israeli Soldier, The Jewish Agency for Israel, POB 92, Jerusalem 91000, Israel; or to: Letter for an Israeli Soldier, Education Department, The Jewish Agency for Israel, 633 Third Avenue 21st Floor, New York, NY 10017.

Also a good idea: "Adopt" a unit or a soldier and send a package by visiting **www.apackagefromhome.org** and following their links.

Sending a Letter to an Israeli Victim

If you're comfortable sending a condolence letter to a victim, go online to the Israeli **Ministry of Foreign Affair**'s website, **www.mfa.gov.il**, and search for "victims." In the pages of victims that appear, click on a name and see if there's a memorial website or contact information to send a letter. Alternatively, you may want to contact an organization in Israel that helps victims and ask them how you can help. Popular ones include **www.natal.org.il** (helping victims with treatments and therapy) and **www.victimsofarabterror.com**.

A Few Resources

- *www.libi-fund.org.il – The Fund for Strengthening Israel's Defense, run by the Ministry of Defense. Online donations are possible.*
- *www.israelsoldiers.org – website of Friends of the IDF, the American partner of the Association for the Wellbeing of Israel's Soldiers (AWIS), which "helps support social, educational and recreational programs and facilities for the young men and women soldiers of Israel who defend the Jewish homeland. We also provide these services to the widows and children of soldiers who have fallen in defense of Israel."*

- *www.mfa.gov.il – Israel's Ministry of Foreign Affairs website, for information, history and updates.*
  For more resources check the resources list in the back of the book.

Praying

One traditional way of showing support is by the simple act of praying. Say a psalm (for example, Psalms 20, 83, or 130), study Torah (if you're Jewish), or go to your local place of worship and ask for a special prayer to be added to the service. I particularly recommend adding a blessing for the welfare of soldiers.

And, incidentally, in this age you can now pray online! If you're Christian, you may want to check out **www.internationalwallof-prayer.org**, **www.c4israel.org**, or **jerusalemprayerteam.org**, to start.

Holding Rallies

Rallies and demonstrations are public expressions of support which garner media attention and notify the politicians, in the strongest way possible, that people really do care about this issue.

They are also broadcast to Israelis, many of whom are holed up in bomb shelters and sincerely appreciate the feeling that they are not alone.

When Israel is under attack, the least we can do is stand for an hour or two in a public square and show our solidarity.

THINGS YOU CAN DO TODAY:

1. Stay informed. Check the news, read updates at **www.mfa.gov.il**, and talk to Israeli contacts.
2. Fly an Israeli flag on your home, car, office, or lapel.
3. Wear a pro-Israel button or t-shirt. Put a bumper sticker on your car.

4. Fight media and political propaganda. Protest bias when you hear it on local or national media – by writing letters, phoning, having e-mail campaigns and talking to advertisers about whom they're supporting.
5. Donate money to Israel (see the chapter **Donating Money and Fundraising Ideas** and the resources list at the back of the book).
6. Send a letter or package to an Israeli soldier.
7. Send a letter to a victim.
8. Send a prayer, if you're so inclined, to help Israel and its soldiers.
9. Speak to your elected representatives about Israel and her fight. Try to speak in person, if possible, for maximum effectiveness.
10. Hold a pro-Israel rally. Advertise it widely.
11. Tell your elected representatives that it's important to you that the government target "charities" that are just front-groups for terrorists. Ask for detailed reports on their progress. Then ask again six months later.
12. Ask your government to go on record with its support.

Appendix

Israel related resources

A word about this list of resources: It isn't meant to be complete, by any means. Nor does the inclusion of a book or a website mean that I endorse its contents. This is simply a list of many of the more popular resources about Israel that are around, many of which can be quite useful and/or entertaining. If there is a resource or website you'd like to submit for a future edition of this book please contact me through the website **www.WaysToHelpIsrael.com**.

ACTIVISM

- **www.israelactivism.com** for some college activism ideas.
- AIPAC (**www.aipac.org**), The American Israel Public Affairs Committee, America's largest pro-Israel lobby.
- Zionist Organization of America (**www.zoa.org**).
- NACPAC (**http://www.nacpac.org**), an American pro-Israel Political Action Committee.
- Professors for a Strong Israel (**www.professors.org.il**).
- Virtual PAC for Israel (**www.vipac.org**), sends e-mails of sample letters for petitioning governments on behalf of Israel.
- Americans for a Safe Israel (**http://www.afsi.org**).
- One Jerusalem (**www.onejerusalem.org**), a foundation advocating that Jerusalem stays the undivided capital of Israel.
- Rinat Yisrael's Israel Action Page (**http://www.rinat.org/israel%20action.htm**), a synagogue's weekly action list on behalf of Israel.
- **www.ou.org/israel/action/israelaction.htm**, for events on behalf of Israel in your area.
- World Union of Jewish Students (**www.wujs.org.il**) has resources for students worldwide.
- Israel Hasbara Committee (**www.infoisrael.net**), for fighting propaganda and for general information.
- Stand With Us (**www.standwithuscampus.com**), for material about Israel, including flyers.
- Campus Watch (**http://www.campus-watch.org**), to report anti-Israel activity on campus.
- Divestment Watch (**http://www.divestmentwatch.com**), to help battle campaigns advocating divestment from Israel.
- Take A Pen (**www.take-a-pen.org**), letter writing campaigns.
- Unity Coalition for Israel (**www.israelunitycoalition.org**), an alliance of Christian and Jewish organizations actively working together to generate support for the State of Israel.
- Hillel (**www.hillel.org**), for college students.

– **www.babaganewz.com**, news about Israel for kids.
– **www.israelcampusbeat.org**.

ANTI-SEMITISM
– Simon Wiesenthal Center (**www.wiesenthal.com**).
– Anti Defamation League (**www.adl.org**).
– Center for Monitoring the Impact of Peace (**www.edume.org**).
– United Kingdom report on anti-Semitism: **www.thepcaa.org/report.htm** and **www.integrationandcohesion.org.uk/Our_final_report.aspx**.
– World Jewish Congress (**www.worldjewishcongress.org/antisemitism.html**).

ARTS AND CULTURE
– **www.jewishwebcasting.com**, links to Israeli media of all sorts.
– **www.ilmuseums.com**, for museums and exhibitions all around Israel.
– **www.israelfilmfestival.com**, Israel Film Festival in the U.S.
– **www.israelartguide.co.il**, for a guide to art in Israel.
– **www.israel-music.com**, for a guide to music in Israel.
– **www.israelidances.com**, for Israeli dances. Links to dance sites worldwide and tells you where you can find an Israeli dance class anywhere in the world.
– For Israeli radio online: **http://bet.iba.org.il** or **www.kol-israel.com**.
– For Israeli radio and TV (mostly in Hebrew): **www.iba.org.il**.
– For Israeli and Jewish songs: **www.hebrewsongs.com**.
– Almagor, Gila. Under the Domim Tree.
– Amichai, Yehuda. The Selected Poetry Of Yehuda Amichai, Newly Revised and Expanded edition (Literature of the Middle East).
– Bialik, Hayyim Nahman. Songs from Bialik: Selected Poems of Hayim Nahman Bialik (Judaic Traditions in Literature, Music, and Art).
– Mazya, Edna. Echoes of Israel. (Collection of plays).
– Oz, Amos. The Story Begins: Essays on Literature.
– Sabato, Haim. Adjusting Sights.
– Yehoshua, A. B. Mr. Mani (Harvest in Translation).

BUSINESS TIES AND ECONOMICS
– Hareshima, The Jewish Internet Portal, (**www.hareshima.com/Israel/Business/Businessdirectory.asp**), links to all sorts of Israeli businesses.
– White Plains for Israel (**www.whiteplainsforIsrael.org**), great links to places to buy Israeli products. Other sites include **www.shopinisrael.com**, **www.export.org.il**, **www.israeliproducts.com**, **http://middleeastfacts.com/mef_buy-israeli-products.php** and **http://www.ou.org/programs/5762/buyisrael.htm**.
– **www.science.co.il**, for links to science related sites in Israel.
– Globes, for Israeli business news (**www.globes-online.com**).
– **www.usaisrael.org**, for American-Israeli business opportunities.
– **www.israelibusinessforum.org**, for Israeli professionals

in the New York area.
- US-Israel Business Exchange (**www.usibex.org**).
- Federation of Israeli Chambers of Commerce
  (**www.chamber.org.il/english**).
- **www.tase.co.il**, for the Tel Aviv Stock Exchange.
- Dun & Bradstreet for Israel (**www.dandb.co.il**).
- **www.jr.co.il/hotsites/i-busin.htm**, for links to many websites of interest.

CHARITY
- Jewish National Fund (**www.jnf.org**).
- UJA-Federation (**www.ujc.org**).
- Joint Distribution Committee (**www.jdc.org**).
- Hadassah (**www.hadassah.org**).
- Magen David Adom (**www.afmda.org**).
- Yad Sarah (for elderly and medical equipment), **www.yadsarah.org**.
- For a very comprehensive list of Israeli non-profits, visit Giving Wisely
  (**www.givingwisely.org.il**).
- The American Society for the Protection of Nature in Israel
  (**www.aspni.org**) – Israel's foremost environment protection agency.

CHRISTIAN ZIONISM
- Christians United For Israel (**www.cufi.org**)
- Bridges For Peace (**www.bridgesforpeace.com**)
- International Christian Embassy Jerusalem (**www.icej.org**)
- International Christian Zionist Center (**www.israelmybeloved.com**)
- **www.patrobertson.com/Speeches/IsraelLauder.asp**
- **www.christianactionforisrael.org**
- **www.christian-zionism.org**
- **www.christiansstandingwithisrael.com**
- **www.zionismontheweb.org**
- **www.c4israel.org**
- **www.cfijerusalem.org**
- **www.cdn-friends-icej.ca**
- **www.ifcj.org**
- **www.pcjcr.org**
- **www.internationalwallofprayer.org**
- **www.c4israel.org**
- **www.jerusalemprayerteam.org**
- Brog, David. Standing with Israel: Why Christians Support
  the Jewish State.
- Campolo, Tony. "The Ideological Roots of Christian Zionism."
  Tikkun magazine, January-February 2005.
- Chafets, Zev. A Match Made in Heaven: American Jews, Christian
  Zionists, and One Man's Exploration of the Weird and Wonderful
  Judeo-Evangelical Alliance.
- Clark, Victoria. Allies for Armageddon: The Rise of Christian Zionism.
- Gorenberg, Gershom. The End of Days: Fundamentalism and the

Struggle for the Temple Mount.
- Hagee, John, In Defense of Israel.
- Oren, Michael B. Power, Faith and Fantasy.

EDUCATIONAL RESOURCES
- Myths & Facts: A guide to the Arab-Israeli Conflict
  (**http://www.jewishvirtuallibrary.org/jsource/myths/mftoc.html**).
  Also exists as a book.
- The Jewish Virtual Library (**www.jewishvirtuallibrary.org**) an
  online encyclopedia of facts.
- Middle East Facts (**http://www.middleeastfacts.com/index.php**).
- Mythbusting the Mideast (**http://www.mythbustingthemideast.com**).
- Israel Info Center (**www.israelinfocenter.com**).
- Middle East Info (**http://www.middle-east-info.org/index.html**,
  particularly for links to maps.
- Israel-Arab Conflict FAQ (**http://www.interall.co.il/israel-faq.html**).
- ConceptWizard (**www.conceptwizard.com/info.html**), a married couple in
  Israel provide info on life there.
- The Golan Heights (**http://www.golan.co.il/borderen.htm**),
  general information on the Golan Heights.
- **www.sixdaywar.org**, for a history of the Six Day War.
- **www.basicjudaism.org**, for a quick overview of Judaism.
  Also check out **www.torah.org**.
- JIMENA: Jews Indigenous to the Middle East and North Africa
  (**www.jimena.org**), historically and currently.
- **http://www.pmo.gov.il/PMOEng**, for the English version of the Israeli
  Prime Minister's office website.
- **http://dover.idf.il/IDF**, the IDF website, in Hebrew.
- **www.eretzyisroel.org/~dhershkowitz**, for photos of Israel in
  the 19th century.
- **http://jic.tau.ac.il/Archive/skins/PalestineP/navigator.asp**,
  for archive issues of the Palestine Post of the 1930's and 40's.
- **www.embassyofisrael.org/kids**, Israel's website for young kids.
- **www.israelhighway.org**, for teens interested in Israel.
- Begin, Menachem. The Revolt.
- Black, Ian and Morris, Benny. Israel's Secret Wars: A History of Israel's
  Intelligence Services.
- Buber, Martin. On Zion: The History of an Idea.
- Collins, Larry and Lapierre, Dominique. O Jerusalem.
- Dershowitz, Alan. The Case for Israel.
- Hertzberg, Arthur. The Zionist Idea: A Historical Analysis and Reader.
- Herzog, Chaim. The Arab-Israeli Wars: War and Peace in the Middle East
  from the War of Independence through Lebanon.
- Oren, Michael B. Six Days of War: June 1967 and the Making of the
  Modern Middle East.
- Rabinovich, Abraham. The Yom Kippur War: The Epic Encounter That
  Transformed the Middle East.

– Sachar, Howard M. A History of Israel: From the Rise of Zionism to Our
  Time, (Second Edition, Revised and Updated).
– Schiff, Ze'ev. Israel's Lebanon War.

INTERFAITH RESOURCES
– **www.interfaith.org.uk**.
– **www.interfaithfamily.com**.

ISRAELI ORGANIZATIONS
– The Movement for Quality Government in Israel
  (**http://www.mqg.org.il/default.htm**), advocating changes in
  Israeli government.
– The Israel Democracy Institute (**http://www.idi.org.il/english**),
  advocating strengthening Israel's democratic institutions.
– The Interdisciplinary Center (Counter-Terrorism) (**www.ict.org.il**),
  Israeli think tank.
– Israel Law Center (**http://www.israellawcenter.org**),
  advocating legal rights.
– The Israel Association for Ethiopian Jews (**www.iaej.org.il/index.htm**).

ISRAELI AND JEWISH ORGANIZATIONS OUTSIDE OF ISRAEL
– First place to look in the U.S.: the local UJA-Federation (UJC) branch, for
  their community network directories with lists of local organizations.
  (**www.ujc.org**).
– Zionist Organization of America (**www.zoa.org**).
– World Jewish Congress (**www.worldjewishcongress.org**).
– AZM, American Zionist Movement (**www.azm.org**), a coalition of groups
  and individuals committed to Zionism. AZM is the American affiliate
  of the World Zionist Organization, the Zionist Federation in the
  United States.
– Hadassah (**www.hadassah.org**).
– AMIT (**www.amitchildren.org**).
– American Jewish Congress (**www.ajcongress.org**).
– World Zionist Organization (**www.wzo.org.il**).
– Bnai Brith (**www.bnaibrith.org**).
– Hillel (**www.hillel.org**).
– Joint Distribution Committee (**www.jdc.org**).
– Jewish National Fund (**www.jnf.org**).
– National Council of Young Israel (**www.youngisrael.org**).
– For many links: **http://pages.infinit.net/jackross/jt-orgs.htm**.

JEWISH OUTREACH
Orthodox:
– Aish HaTorah (**www.aish.com**).
– Chabad (**www.chabad.org**).
– National Jewish Outreach Program (**www.njop.org**).
– Gateways (**www.gatewaysonline.com**).

- Ohr Somayach (**www.ohr.edu**).
- Jewish Media Resources (**www.jewishmediaresources.com**), for journalists looking for the Orthodox perspective about Israel.

Conservative:
- Kehillah (**www.ikehillah.org**).
- KOACH (**www.koach.org**).

Reform:
- Jewish Outreach Institute (**www.joi.org**).
- Reform Jewish Outreach (**www.urj.org/outreach**).

MONITORING MEDIA AND ORGANIZATIONS
- MEMRI (**www.memri.org**), The Middle East Media Research Institute, especially for translations of Middle East press.
- CAMERA (**www.camera.org**), The Committee for Accuracy in Middle East Reporting in America.
- Honest Reporting (**www.honestreporting.com**), tracks reporting of Israel in the international media.
- Eye on the UN, (**www.eyeontheun.org**).
- UN Watch, (**www.unwatch.org**), monitoring the United Nations and promoting human rights.
- Palestinian Media Watch (**www.pmw.org.il**), keeping an eye on the Palestinian Authority and its organs.
- NGO Monitor (**http://www.ngo-monitor.org**).
- Primer Action Center (**http://tampabayprimer.org**), keeping an eye on the media.
- Behind the News in Israel (**http://www.israelbehindthenews.com**), David Bedein's website examining news and media.

TRAVELING TO ISRAEL
- **www.birthright.org**, for free trips to Israel, if you're eligible.
- **www.destinationisrael.com/Scholarships.asp**, for scholarship possibilities to travel to Israel.
- **www.kibbutzprogramcenter.org**, for Kibbutz possibilities and programs.
- **www.goisrael.com**, tours and itineraries.
- **www.planetware.com/israel-tourism-vacations-isr.htm**, for tourist vacations.
- **www.itastours.com**, tours and bar/bat mitzvah packages.
- Discover Israel (**www.ddtravel-acc.com**).
- For volunteering in the IDF, short term: **www.sar-el.org**, or **www.wzo.org.il/en/programs/view.asp?id=120** (marva).
- For a list of programs to volunteer in: **www.ivolunteer.org.il/Eng/Index.asp?CategoryID=125**.
- For Aliyah: **www.jewishagency.org/JewishAgency/English/Aliyah** or **Nefesh b'Nefesh** (**www.nbn.org.il**), or **AACI** (**www.aaci.org.il**) or **British Olim Society** (**www.ujia.org.il**), or **Tehilla** (**www.tehilla.com**) and check out

www.jr.co.il/aliyah/olimorg.htm for more organizations and phone numbers.
- To learn Hebrew at an Ulpan in Israel: **www.ulpanor.com**, **www.ulpan-akiva.org**, **www.jafi.org.il/aliyah/abscenters/abscentlist/ulpanetzion/index.asp** or check out a comprehensive list at **www.nbn.org.il/learn_hebrew/ulpan_listing.htm**.

YOUTH GROUPS & SUMMER CAMPS
- BBYO, B'nai B'rith Youth Organization, (**www.bbyo.org**).
- Bnai Akiva, a religious Zionist movement (**www.bneiakiva.org**).
- Ami Chai youth movement (**www.amichaiusa.com**).
- North American Federation of Temple Youth (**www.nfty.org**)
- United Synagogue Youth (**www.usy.org**).
- Betar Zionist Youth Movement (**www.betar.org**).
- National Conference for Synagogue Youth (**www.ncsy.org**).
- Young Judea (Hadassah) at **www.youngjudaea.org**.
- Hareshima, The Jewish Internet Portal, (**www.hareshima.com/Organizations/summercamps.ASP**) for more camps.

WAR RELATED RESOURCES
- **www.libi-fund.org.il**, for helping Israeli soldiers.
- Friends of the Israel Defense Forces, **www.israelsoldiers.org**.
- NATAL – Israel Center for Victims of Terror and War (**http://www.natal.org.il**), organization treating Israeli victims of terror and war.
- ADL Database of International Terrorism (**http://www.adl.org/main_Terrorism/default.htm**), for news and articles on international terrorism.
- Foreign Ministry Online: Films on Terrorism (**http://w3.castup.net/mfa/terror.htm**), Israeli Government collection of films on terrorism.
- Internet Haganah (**http://haganah.org.il**), confronting Jihad on the internet.
- Israeli Foreign Ministry site in memory of victims (**www.mfa.gov.il**).
- Terrorism Questions and Answers (**http://cfrterrorism.org/home**).
- Victims of Arab Terror (**www.victimsofarabterror.org**).
- Kids for Kids (**www.kidsforkids.net**), for kids to help Israeli children who are victims.
- We Should Not Forget (**http://www.jr.co.il/terror/israel/index.html**), memorial for victims; updated often.
- Crisis or Challenge (**http://www.crisis.org.il**), a practical guide to coping with bereavement, stress and modern day terror.

About the Author

Haskell Nussbaum holds degrees in physics and law, the latter from the Hebrew University of Jerusalem. He served as a judicial clerk to a Justice of the Supreme Court of Israel, and in the Golani Infantry Brigade of the Israel Defense Forces. He has contributed articles and stories to the Jerusalem Report, Pacific News Service, the Canadian Jewish News, Moment, the Jewish Week, HaModia and others.

Nussbaum is also the author of **Beat That Parking Ticket, A Complete Guide for New York City**, a comprehensive behind-the-scenes guide to fighting parking tickets.

Nussbaum has been featured in New York Magazine's Daily Intelligencer, USA Today, the New York Post, Metro, the Jewish Week and other magazines and newspapers and has appeared on radio and TV shows such as NPR, Fox & Friends, Today in New York, NY1, CBS Evening News, Good Day New York and many others.

In addition to being an attorney, Nussbaum has also worked as an adjunct professor at Touro College in New York.

Nussbaum can be reached at Nussbaum@WaysToHelpIsrael.com.